W9-BSG-600

THE

[E S S E N T I A L
J E S U S]

100 READINGS THROUGH THE BIBLE'S GREATEST STORY

W H I T N E Y T. K U N I H O L M

IVP Connect

An imprint of InterVarsity Press
Downers Grove, Illinois

InterVarsity Press
P.O. Box 1400, Downers Grove, IL 60515-1426
World Wide Web: www.ivpress.com
E-mail: email@ivpress.com

InterVarsity Press® is the book-publishing division of InterVarsity Christian Fellowship/USA®, a movement of students and faculty active on campus at hundreds of universities, colleges and schools of nursing in the United States of America, and a member movement of the International Fellowship of Evangelical Students. For information about local and regional activities, write Public Relations Dept., InterVarsity Christian Fellowship/USA, 6400 Schroeder Rd., P.O. Box 7895, Madison, WI 53707-7895, or visit the IVCF website at <www.intervarsity.org>.

All Scripture quotations, unless otherwise indicated, are taken from the Holy Bible, New International Version®. NIV®. Copyright ©1973, 1978, 1984 by International Bible Society. Used by permission of Zondervan Publishing House. All rights reserved.

Images: Crosssection Photographer: Beerlogoff (shutterstock)

ISBN 978-0-8308-1098-7

Printed in the United States of America ∞

Library of Congress Cataloging-in-Publication Data

Kuniholm, Whitney, T.
  The essential Jesus: 100 readings through the Bible's greatest
story for individuals and groups / Whitney T. Kuniholm.
     p. cm.
  ISBN-13: 978-0-8308-1098-7 (pbk.: alk. paper)
  1. Jesus Christ—Person and offices—Devotional literature. I.
Title.
  BT205.K83 2007
  232—dc22

                                                              2007031447

P   22   21   20   19   18   17   16   15   14   13   12   11   10   9

Y   29   28   27   26   25   24   23   22   21   20   19   18

CONTENTS

INTRODUCTION

"If Jesus was the most influential person in history, I'd like to learn more about him."

"I know people have strong opinions about Jesus, and that's fine. But I'd like to find out for myself what he said and did so I can come to my own conclusions."

"Of course I know who Jesus is; who doesn't? I've just never taken the time to read all that the Bible says about him."

"I've heard people say, 'I'm a follower of Jesus.' But what does that really mean?"

COMMENTS ABOUT JESUS

NO MATTER WHAT YOU THINK ABOUT JESUS, there's no denying he is the most influential person in all of human history. And what's truly amazing is that his path to influence was so unlikely.

Jesus never became a political, military or government leader; he never wanted to. He never owned a multinational corporation or acquired any wealth to speak of; he didn't need it. He never wrote a book, never staged a concert tour, never appeared on television and never had a radio talk show or even his own blog. He was born in a barn, grew up as a laborer, remained single and childless his entire life, and was executed at the age of thirty-three.

Yet somehow Jesus became the reference point for life ever since—we mark our calendars by his death. He has inspired some of the world's greatest art, literature, music and architecture. His ethical teachings have been hailed as the world's greatest—even by those who aren't his followers. He's been the subject of countless books, articles, television programs and movies. Today his church has more members than any other religion in the world—and persecution only makes it grow larger. Not only that, the book that gives us the most information about him—the Bible—has sold more copies than any volume ever printed. What's so special about Jesus?

That's what I hope you'll discover in *The Essential Jesus*. We'll take an honest look at what Jesus said and did so we can determine who he really was and is. To do this, we'll read and reflect on one hundred carefully selected passages from the Bible. And we'll approach our journey not as theological experts but as open-minded seekers who want to get a true understanding of the most influential person in history. Are you ready?

THE BIBLE'S GREATEST STORY

Most people have a basic knowledge of the Bible. They know it describes how God created the world and how he has been involved with it ever since. Not only that, they've read some of the Bible's most popular stories, like the account of Adam and Eve in the Garden of Eden, and of Abraham and the birth of Israel, and Moses and the exodus, David and Goliath, Jonah and the whale, Daniel in the lion's den, Peter on day of Pentecost, and Paul on the road to Damascus.

But the one story people seem to know the best is the story of Jesus. Every Christmas we hear the familiar account of Joseph and Mary traveling to the little town of Bethlehem, of Jesus' birth in a manger and of the angels singing "Glory to God in the highest, and on earth peace, good will toward men" (Luke 2:14 KJV). But why is that story more important than all the rest? Because, as you'll see, Jesus is the focal point of God's plan to save the world from sin and to offer people eternal life. The greatest story in the Bible is Jesus; from Genesis to Revelation the Bible is literally "his story."

So as we follow the story line of Jesus through the Old and New Testaments, we'll not only get a clear understanding of the essential Jesus, but we'll also get a good overview of the Bible. Here's how the hundred readings are organized.

Who is Jesus? We'll begin our journey with five readings from some contemporaries of Jesus: two of his disciples, Peter and John, and the apostle Paul, a man who had a unique encounter with Jesus soon after his resurrection. Each of these five readings gives us a soaring description of Jesus and his significance. They are some of the most inspiring and memorable passages in the Bible, and together they form a sort of prologue to our exploration of the essential Jesus.

The Old Testament. Our next twenty-five readings take us to the Old Testament, because the story of Jesus began long before the manger. In the very first book in the Bible we get our first indication that God was planning to send a Messiah, a Savior for the world, which raises an obvious question: Why do we need a Savior? Once we come to grips with the answer (hint: the answer is sin!), we'll then trace what the Bible says about this coming Savior in the Psalms and in the Prophets. You'll be amazed at how much the Old Testament has to say about this coming Savior and how perfectly Jesus matched the picture God had been describing for centuries.

The New Testament. The longest part of our journey, sixty-five readings in all, will follow the story about Jesus in the New Testament. We'll read the accounts of Jesus found in the four Gospels: Matthew, Mark, Luke and John. We'll examine his birth, ministry, teaching, miracles, death, resurrection and the church. And we'll explore the unfinished part of his story, that is, the time in the future when Jesus will return to earth for all those who believe in him. By this point in the journey, you'll have a complete picture of the essential Jesus.

Who is Jesus . . . to you? In the final five readings, you'll get an opportunity to do something really important: form your own opinion about Jesus. To help, we'll consider several people who came face to face with Jesus. Some rejected him; some embraced him. But in each case you'll see that Jesus challenged people to respond. Why? Because his desire is to have a relationship with every human being, including you. That was God's plan from the beginning, and it's why Jesus came to earth.

MY STORY

Before we go any further, there are two things I want to clarify. First, even though I am a committed follower of Jesus Christ myself, I'm not going to force my beliefs on you. What you believe is your responsibility. What I hope to do in this book is guide you through the Bible so that you can come to your own conclusion about Jesus. Second, as we take this journey together, I'm also going to share some of my personal experiences and observations. I've learned that both the Bible and all of life can teach us about Jesus.

So now that you know where I'm coming from, let me tell you how my relationship with Jesus began.

I grew up in a Christian home and spent lots of time at church, Sunday school and Christian camps, so I can't remember a time when I didn't know about Jesus. But I can remember the first time I consciously said yes to being his follower. I was six years old and sitting in a Sunday night church service led by my father. At the end of the program he asked everyone to close their eyes and then said something like, "If anyone wants to give their heart to Jesus, I want you to raise your hand right now." I didn't really understand everything he was saying. All I knew is that I wanted to give my life to Jesus. So I raised my hand.

By the time I got to college many years later, I began to wonder, *Do I really believe what I accepted as a child?* One thing that especially bothered me was that I seemed to know a lot about the Christian faith, but I didn't seem to feel much. How could I determine if my faith was real? During that time, I went to a week-long series of evangelistic meetings. At the end, the preacher asked people to come forward and make a public commitment to follow Jesus. This created dilemma for me. I was now old enough to make my own decisions, but I already believed in Jesus, or at least I thought I did. *Can a Christian get saved?* I wondered.

Feeling unsure, I walked to the front hoping that some wise person would counsel me through my question. But no one joined me at the altar rail. Everyone was busy praying with others. So I quietly whispered the shortest prayer I've ever prayed: *Thank you, Jesus.* That's all I said, and then I began to cry, to really sob, and it lasted for quite a while.

Again, I didn't really understand what was happening, but I believe that God, in his mercy, was letting me know that he could not only touch my mind, but he could touch my heart as well. Today, whenever I take Communion in church, I always whisper that prayer as I walk back to my seat, *Thank you Jesus.* It's my way of affirming that I'm still his follower.

That's how it happened for me. But the fact is, everyone has a different experience. Some people struggle with the decision to follow Jesus. Others come to it more easily. The most important thing is that you find out who Jesus is and then come to your own conclusion about him. I believe that's the most important decision you'll ever make.

HOW TO USE *THE ESSENTIAL JESUS*

At this point you may be thinking something like this: *Hold on. I'm interested in Jesus but I can't read the Bible! It's too long and confusing.* If so, don't worry; most people feel that way. That's why I've designed this book to make your journey through the Bible easy and meaningful. Let me begin by making a few suggestions that will get you off to a good start.

First, *The Essential Jesus* is designed to be used—with a Bible. It tells you what Bible passage to read and then helps you reflect on the main points. Obviously without reading each Bible passage, *The Essential Jesus* won't make much sense. Also be sure to use a translation of the Bible that is easy for you to read. Although the King James Version (KJV) is beautiful and widely available, it is often difficult for modern readers to understand since it was translated into the language of 1611. I recommend that you use one of the many excellent modern translations such as the New International Version (NIV), New Living Translation (NLT) or the Contemporary English Version (CEV). If you are still unsure about which Bible translation to use, you might want to check with a pastor, minister or priest.

Second, *The Essential Jesus* guides you through one hundred short Bible passages, all of which relate to Jesus. The readings are undated, so you can complete them at any pace—one hundred days, six months, a year or more. But whatever schedule you pick, don't feel guilty if you miss a day (trust me, you will). Just do the next reading whenever you have time, and before you know it you'll make it through all one hundred. I've also grouped the readings into sets of five that begin with an introduction that alerts you to important themes. You might try to do one set of five readings each week.

Third, you will notice that for each reading I've followed a five-step format—Pray, Read, Reflect, Apply, Pray—one you can use anytime you read the Bible. In the Bible, God speaks to you. In prayer, you can respond to him. So by integrating the two, you can have a regular dialogue with God. Here are some additional ideas on how to get the most out of the five steps:

• Pray before you read, asking God to help you understand his Word to you. The written prayer will get you started, but feel free to add thanksgiving, confession, praise or whatever you'd like to express to God. Remember, you're beginning a dialogue.

• Read carefully the Bible passage. If you have time, you may want to read the passage more than once or review the surrounding passages for context. Also keep a pencil or highlighter handy so you can make notes or underline key phrases or verses.

• Reflect on what you've read. First, summarize your own observations on the passage either mentally or in a notebook or journal. It may help to ask: What was the main point of this passage? Which verses relate to my life now? Then think further about the passage by reading my reflections.

• Apply what God teaches you from his Word to your life. Take some time to think this through. Did the passage contain an example to follow, a warning to heed, a promise to claim? How should this affect your thoughts, words and actions? You might want to jot down how you'd like to apply these things in your life.

• Pray again, asking God to help you live out his Word. This time, turn the things you've learned into prayers. Also pray about your own needs and the needs of others. And be sure to thank God for any answers to prayer.

DON'T GO IT ALONE

At the end of each section, I've included a page of discussion questions. Why? Because *the best way to use this book* is to read it with another person, or to use it as the basis of a group study. Each week, try to complete a set of five readings on your own. Then get together with your friend or group to talk about what you've learned. Start by encouraging each person to share their own insights from the readings. Then use the discussion questions to help you continue your conversation. You'll find that reading the Bible with others creates a positive motivation to keep going and makes your experience of God's Word more meaningful.

Another idea you may want to consider is "The Essential Jesus Challenge," a program from Scripture Union that enables an entire church or group to read what the Bible says about Jesus using this book together. (To learn more, see page 199 or go to www.EssentialJesusChallenge.com.)

YOUR HIGHER GOAL

From beginning to end, the Bible tells the story of how "God so loved the world that he gave his one and only Son, that whoever believes in him shall not perish but have eternal life" (John 3:16). So as you begin your journey through the greatest story in the Bible, keep in mind that your goal is not just to make it to one hundred or to gain more Bible knowledge or even to develop greater spiritual discipline. Those things are important, but your higher goal is to get to know Jesus. The secret to making the Bible come alive is to view reading it as an opportunity to have an encounter with the risen Christ, the one who loves you, who died for you and who desires to have a living relationship with you.

My prayer is that over the next few months the Bible's greatest story will come alive for you as never before. But don't let *The Essential Jesus* be the end of your engagement with the Bible. Let this journey become the beginning of a lifetime adventure of meeting God every day in the Bible and prayer.

PART ONE

Who Is Jesus?

WHAT IS THE MOST IMPORTANT QUESTION in all of human history?

Of course, everyone is curious about their own existence: Who am I? Where did I come from? Where am I going? In addition, many wonder about the great challenges in the world today: How can we stop war and maintain peace? How can we cure various diseases? How can we eliminate poverty? How can we protect the environment?

But I'm convinced there is one question more important than all the rest: Who is Jesus? Why? Because Jesus claimed he was God on the earth. That's right; he said he was God's promised Messiah, the one and only Savior of the world. And if that's true, really true, then everything else is secondary.

When you think about it, our world is full of information about Jesus—in movies and plays, on television and radio, and in magazines and books. Some of it is accurate, some not. Often he's positioned as the founder of a religion—Christianity. Other times he's portrayed as a moral teacher, a miracle worker or a martyr. Some see him as a revolutionary, a charlatan or a curse. There are even some who don't think he existed at all; they think the stories of Jesus are legends and myths.

So how do we find out who the essential Jesus really is? The best way is to go to the most complete source of information we have about him, the Bible. As you read through the hundred passages about Jesus that I've selected, you'll quickly see that the story line of Jesus is the "scarlet thread" that runs through the Bible from beginning to end. Jesus is what the Bible is all about.

In our first five readings, we'll consider the thoughts of three people who were close to Jesus: John and Peter, two of his key disciples, and Paul, who had a unique encounter with Jesus. Each of these readings describes Jesus in the loftiest terms. Later in our journey we'll get to the particulars of his life. But for now, we need to get the big picture, and that's where we'll start.

1 ∾ TRUTH BEYOND FACTS

PRAY: Dear God, I'm on a mission to find out who Jesus really is. Please open the eyes of my heart so I can take an honest look at him.

READ: John 1:1-18

REFLECT: Journalists think of their profession as a quest for truth: If they accurately report all the facts of a story, then they believe they've told the whole truth. But as John begins his account of the life of Jesus, he realizes the truth goes far beyond mere facts. The man he lived alongside for three years was divine and human at the same time. How do you describe a truth like that?

The other Gospel writers start with the practical details of Jesus' life—who his ancestors were (Matthew), how his public ministry got started (Mark) and how he was born (Luke). John starts by calling Jesus "the Word," a curious phrase but one that captures something important. Jesus was a statement from God to humankind: If you want to know who I am, look at Jesus. Why? Because "the Word was God" (v. 1). Not just a great teacher or healer, celebrity or leader. The essential truth about Jesus is that he was God on earth (v. 14).

That's a pretty bold claim. But if it's true, what difference does it make?

First, Jesus is a *new source of light* in the world (vv. 5-9). John uses the image of light and darkness to describe Jesus' mission. A world without God is a sinful, dark place. If you need proof, just turn on your television.

When Jesus appeared, it was like a candle in a dark room; people could finally see a way to God.

Second, Jesus is the *source of new life* (vv. 4, 12). If there is no God, if there is no afterlife, then there is no meaning; death is the end. But Jesus offered a way out of such futility. He invites everyone to be part of God's family forever (v. 12). How sad that some aren't interested (vv. 10-11).

As we begin to explore what the Bible says about Jesus, we need to remember that the facts tell only part of the story. The truth about Jesus doesn't contradict the facts. It's just far, far bigger.

APPLY: Has God ever communicated with you? How? How did you respond?

PRAY: Jesus, as I learn more about you, I'd also like to experience more of you in my life. I ask for your help with . . .

2 ❧ LIVING LIKE JESUS

PRAY: Heavenly Father, in the midst of my busy, stressful life, I want to be still, just for a few minutes so I can hear from you.

READ: Philippians 2:1-11

REFLECT: During the 1960s there was something of a revival of interest in Jesus in the West. In a decade of radical change, he seemed like an ideal role model. Young men even tried to look like him; they had long hair, grew beards and even wore leather sandals (a classmate of mine called them "Jesus boots"). But what does it mean to live like Jesus? That's the issue we'll consider today.

Actually, there was a specific situation the apostle Paul was addressing in this passage: he wanted the Christians in a first-century city called Philippi to be less selfish and more loving, compassionate, joyful and united (vv. 1-4). Good advice for Christians in any town, at any time. But the question was how? Paul's answer was simple: live like Jesus. He proceeds to give one of the most soaring descriptions of Jesus in the entire Bible (vv. 5-11). Let's unpack what he says and how we can apply it to our lives:

- *Jesus is God* (v. 6). Ever since Paul had an encounter with the risen Christ (Acts 9:1-9), he was a fearless witness for his Lord. Are you?

- *Jesus became a human being* (vv. 7-8). He wasn't a spiritual Casper the Ghost. He came and lived with us (John 1:14). How real is Jesus to you?

- *Jesus humbled himself* (v. 7). The Creator of the universe was willing to serve his creatures. Are you willing to serve those "lower" than you?

- *Jesus obeyed his Father* (v. 8). For him it meant death on the cross. What does obeying God mean for you today?

- *Jesus was exalted by God* (v. 9). The way God did it was to bring Jesus back to life. Are you convinced that Jesus is alive today?

- *Jesus will be acknowledged by everyone* (vv. 10-11). No matter what you believe about him now, one day you'll come face to face with Jesus. What will you say when you do?

Whether it's the first century, the 1960s or today, living like Jesus begins with a decision to follow the One who "became obedient to death— even death on a cross" (v. 8). Now *that's* a radical idea.

APPLY: What is one thing you could do to sacrificially serve someone close to you this week?

PRAY: Imagine that you are face to face with Jesus right now. What do you want to say?

3 ❧ IT'S ALL ABOUT JESUS

PRAY: God, I ask that you would open my eyes to see something new about your Son today.

READ: Colossians 1:15-23

REFLECT: For a long time, we had several cans of concentrated grape juice in our pantry. It looked like regular grape juice, but if we forgot it was concentrate and tried to drink straight from the can, we'd have a hard time swallowing it.

In a way, that's what our passage today is like; it's concentrated truth about Jesus, and you may have had a hard time swallowing everything you read. That's okay. The reason we're covering this passage now is that in just a few verses it introduces us to several of the major themes about Jesus that we'll be exploring in our journey through the Bible.

The book of Colossians was written by the apostle Paul to counteract the impact some false teachers were having on the new believers in the city of Colossae. These teachers had devised complicated schemes to describe how people should relate to God. It sounded impressive, but something important was missing: Jesus. Theology, teaching and our view of the church are vital to Christian faith. But if Jesus is not at the center of them all, they've missed the point.

To correct the problem, Paul offers a concentrated description of Jesus that echoes some of the things we've already discovered. The main point is that Jesus is God (vv. 15, 19; see also Colossians 2:9), and he is woven into the fabric of all creation (vv. 16-17). Paul builds on this foundation with two new insights that add to our picture of Jesus. First, Jesus is *the head of the church* (v. 18). If you eliminate the head, the body dies. Second, Jesus is *the key to the good news* (vv. 20-23). Without him, we are still alienated from God.

Churches today are still plagued by false teaching. Instead of wasting energy attacking or arguing, we would do well to follow Paul's example; he started with the positive (Colossians 1:3-14), and then says, in effect, "Let's get back to basics. It's all about Jesus."

APPLY: In your opinion, what are "the basics" about Jesus? Are there any claims about Jesus that you've found hard to swallow?

PRAY: Thank you God that you made a way for me to have a relationship with you, and that way is Jesus.

4 ∿ WHAT IS GOD LIKE?

PRAY: Dear God, I'm hungry to know you better, thirsty to experience you more.

READ: Hebrews 1:1-4

REFLECT: I once saw a video of young children being asked a simple question: "What is God like?" I chuckled when the first adorable child looked straight into the camera, smiled and answered, "I don't know." They asked another child who shrugged and said, "Don't know." And another, "Don't know." Several more gave the same answer. The last child just shook her head and looked down.

What *is* God like? No matter how old you are, that's not an easy question. But the writer to the Hebrews (we don't know who it was) has the best answer. If you want to know what God is like, look at Jesus; he's the "exact representation" of God (v. 3). Want to know what God thinks about the world? Look at Jesus. Want to know what God likes and dislikes? Look at Jesus. What to know what God thinks about people or about you? Look at Jesus.

The book of Hebrews will go on to cover all kinds of issues that were important to the first Jewish Christians, as well as to us. But it starts with an important fact: God has always wanted people to know who he is, and he's been saying so for centuries (v. 1). But in Jesus, God goes even further. He shows up himself and says, "Look! *This* is who I am."

And make no mistake. Although Jesus was human, he was no ordinary guy. He was an expression of God's glory (also see John 8:54), who died for sins, came to life and returned to his place in heaven (Hebrews 1:3). That's the gospel in a nutshell. As we pursue the essential Jesus through the pages of the Bible, we will confront a man like no other, who is a God like no other.

APPLY: How would you describe what God is like? How could you communicate that to someone this week?

PRAY: Heavenly Father, I'm so thankful that you want me to know who you are. In spite of all my distractions, that's my heart's desire.

5 ✎ THE BIG CHURCH

PRAY: It's so good, heavenly Father, to spend time reading and reflecting on your Word. Please show me something new about your Son Jesus today.

READ: 1 Peter 2:4-10

REFLECT: Have you ever heard someone say, "Jesus is my personal Lord and Savior"? No doubt people who say that are sincere and want us to know of their deep commitment to following Jesus. That's a good thing. But to some, the statement sounds a little exclusive, as if the Christian faith is about "me and Jesus, and no one else."

In our passage today, the apostle Peter opens our eyes to another important truth about Jesus: saying yes to following him makes us part of a big group called the church. We'll unpack this idea later in our journey (especially in the section titled "The Early Church of Jesus"), but for now let's try to get the basic concept.

To describe the church, Peter uses a picture of bricks and mortar, but gives it a new spiritual meaning. The church is like a "spiritual house" (v. 5) made up of Jesus ("the living Stone" [v. 4]) and his followers ("living stones" [v. 5]). In other words, the church is not a physical building; it's a "people belonging to God" (v. 9), with Jesus Christ as its cornerstone (v. 6). And he's not a lifeless, granite memorial from the past. Jesus is alive and present in his church today (v. 4). Those who reject that fact will stumble and fall (vv. 4, 7-8). But all those who choose to follow Jesus—past, present and future—become like him and are connected to each other (v. 5).

The church I attend used to meet in an old building of gray stone. Over the years the congregation has grown, so recently we had to expand the facilities. When the new building was finally completed we saw that one of the walls had been built around a large stone cross. It makes a lasting statement about what we believe: this church is built around Jesus Christ. That's exactly what the apostle Peter is saying in this passage, only the church he's referring to is much, much bigger.

APPLY: Are you one of "the living stones" in God's "spiritual house"? How do you know?

PRAY: Spend some time praying for the church you attend most often. Ask God to give you a deeper understanding of what it means to be a "living stone" in the big church.

DISCUSSION QUESTIONS FOR "WHO IS JESUS?"

1. What would you say is the most common understanding about Jesus today? That is, what does "the average person" believe about Jesus?

2. What have you learned about Jesus from movies, plays, television or novels? How is Jesus portrayed in popular culture?

3. How and when did you first learn about Jesus? Has your understanding of Jesus changed over the years? If so, how?

4. How would you describe your view of Jesus today?

5. Do you think it matters what people believe about Jesus? Why?

6. Do you think Christians should actively try to persuade non-Christians to believe in Jesus? Why or why not?

7. Do you think Jesus is different than any other of the world's great religious leaders? If so, how?

PART TWO

Old Testament

The Need for a Savior

THE BIBLE TEACHES THAT JESUS is the Savior of the world. But that raises an obvious question: Why do we need to be saved? What problem is so great that God himself had to come to earth to solve it? In a word, the problem is sin, and that's the theme of our next five passages.

We'll begin by reading the account of "the first sin," when Adam and Eve disobeyed God in the Garden of Eden. The idea of a talking serpent might seem comical to modern readers. Who's ever seen a talking snake? But the reality of Satan and evil is not funny at all.

Next, we'll consider a classic example of how sin spreads from an individual to a community, as we read how the people of Israel worshiped a golden calf. We can only imagine how different things would have been if Aaron would have responded to the request for an alternative god by saying, "No way!" Simple though it may sound, just saying no is still a good strategy for avoiding sin today.

We'll finish the section by reading a few examples of what the psalmist and the prophets had to say about sin. And guess what? It's not positive; we'll come face to face with God's angry side. He really doesn't like sin at all.

Some people wonder if all the talk about sin is unnecessarily negative. Doesn't it just make us feel guilty? Who needs that? Wouldn't it be better to focus on the positive themes in the Bible, like peace and love? Not really. Sin isn't something we can avoid, like a bad hair day, if we're careful. Rather, sin is more like a congenital heart defect; we're born with it.

The good news is that Jesus came to fix our sin problem. But before that can happen, we need to understand our problem. We need to understand why we need a Savior in the first place.

6 ∾ It's Sin!

PRAY: Lord God, I'm hungry for a closer relationship with you. Enable me to sense your presence as I reflect on your Word.

READ: Genesis 3:1-24

REFLECT: I grew up as the oldest of four children. That meant I was expected to be a good influence on my siblings. Sometimes it worked out that way and sometimes . . . let's just say I had a different agenda. So when my mom reached the boiling point with me, she'd play her ultimate trump card: "If you do that again," she'd say with conviction, "it's *sin!*"

But what exactly is sin, and where did it come from? That's the question this passage answers for us. Adam and Eve had the perfect life—no work, no worries, no problems. All they had to do is obey one simple rule, and paradise was theirs forever (Genesis 2:16-17). It sounds easy, but it's not. There's something about human nature that draws us to disobey God's rules (Romans 7:7-25). As a young child I once stomped up the stairs holding my ears, shouting back at my parents, "If you say no, that means I *have* to do it!"

We tend to think sin is some obvious evil act, like murdering or stealing, and of course, that's part of it. But the full picture is more subtle and dangerous. Note that the serpent doesn't ask Eve to reject God. He simply questions God's authority (Genesis 3:1) and contradicts God's word (v. 4). Honest questions and even doubts can help us grow in our faith. But questioning God's authority or living in contradiction to what he says in the Bible is a different matter. That *is* sin.

And sin has consequences, as we see in this passage—shame (v. 7), fear (v. 10), pain (v. 16) and death (v. 19). But the worst consequence is a broken relationship with God; we're banished from his presence (v. 23), doomed to live with a God-shaped hole in our hearts and unable to reestablish a relationship with him on our own (v. 24). No wonder we need a Savior.

APPLY: How would you define sin? How do you deal with it in your life?

PRAY: Heavenly Father, it's hard to recognize and harder still to admit, but it's true: I need a Savior.

7 ∿ STUPID SIN

PRAY: "Speak Lord, for your servant is listening" (1 Samuel 3:9-10).

READ: Exodus 32:1—33:6

REFLECT: How could they be so stupid? The Israelites had witnessed God at work ever since he miraculously released them from bondage in Egypt. Yet they can't wait for Moses to return with the Ten Commandments. In their impatience, they whip each other up into a frenzy of hedonism and pagan worship. It's a poignant reminder about the nature of sin. No matter how good we've been in the past, we're never immune from sin's influence in the present.

Think about Aaron. In some ways, you can't fault him—all he did was give the people what they wanted (Exodus 32:1-2). That's what political leaders are supposed to do, right? The problem is, Aaron was a *spiritual* leader; his actions affected the moral and religious life of the community. The truth is, all of us are spiritual leaders, even if we aren't ordained or aren't particularly religious. Our actions influence the moral decisions of others, for good or for ill.

In contrast, think of the influence Moses had on the people of Israel. He certainly wasn't the life of the party (Exodus 32:19-20, 25-29). He took a strong stand against the idolatry and wild behavior he saw all around. Today it may seem enlightened to believe that sin "ain't nobody's business but my own." The problem is, that's not true. Ultimately our sin is God's business; it's his commands that we violate (Exodus 32:8) and his consequences we must pay (Exodus 32:33-34). Again it highlights our need, our desperate need, for a Savior.

But even in the middle of this out-of-control situation, we see a wonderful example of God's plan for dealing with our sin problem. Moses volunteers to take the punishment the people deserved (Exodus 32:31-32); he was willing to make what we call "atonement" (satisfying the requirements to restore our relationship with God [Exodus 32:30]). That's exactly what Jesus did on the cross thousands of years later.

APPLY: Who has been the greatest influence you your life? Whose life have you influenced the most? In both cases, what was the influence?

PRAY: Dear Jesus, I can't thank you enough for what you did on the cross. Thanks for your willingness to take my punishment.

8 ❧ NOT JUST THE BAD GUYS

PRAY: Heavenly Father, help me to understand more about the sin problem as I read your Word today.

READ: Psalm 14:1-7

REFLECT: Years ago, my wife and I made friends with a couple who wouldn't go to church. They were committed to their marriage, were loving parents and were involved in the community. But they were firm in their resistance to organized religion. Why? They didn't want to damage their son's self-esteem by exposing him to any talk about sin.

It would be nice if sin only affected the "bad guys" of the world, those who deny God (v. 1) and aggressively pursue an evil agenda (v. 4). There's no doubt it does; we only have to read the daily news to see evidence of that. But David says sin also affects the "good guys." We've all "turned aside"; we're all "corrupt." No one is good, "not even one" (v. 3).

That may seem harsh or negative at first, especially for those who identify themselves with the "good guys." But if sin affects everyone, as David states, then it's not healthy to deny its hold on us. And that's why a good church is so important. Like a hospital, it doesn't give us the problem; it helps us diagnose and deal with it.

But it's important not to let our understanding of sin cause us to misunderstand God. It's true, he hates sin. But it's not true that he enjoys catching people in their sins, as so many seem to think. In fact, his desire for us is just the opposite. He's actively looking for those who are seeking a deeper relationship with him (v. 2).

David ends his psalm with a prayer for a savior. "Oh, that salvation would come out to Zion!" (v. 7). God answered that prayer centuries later when he sent his Son, Jesus Christ, to restore all people from captivity to sin. That's reason to rejoice and be glad!

APPLY: How do you picture God? What do you want most from him?

PRAY: Dear God, in spite of all my inconsistencies, I do desire a deeper relationship with you. Help me to understand you better and experience you more.

9 ❧ He's Against It

PRAY: Dear Lord, I ask that you would strengthen my relationship with you as I spend time in your Word.

READ: Isaiah 59:1-21

REFLECT: President Calvin Coolidge was famous for giving short answers. It is reported that he was once questioned about a church service he had attended and allegedly answered as follows. Question: "Did you like the sermon today?" Coolidge: "Yes." Question: "What was the sermon about?" Coolidge: "Sin." Question: "So, what did the preacher say about sin?" Coolidge: "He's against it."

This reading from Isaiah reminds us once again that God is against sin. That means we should be too, for several important reasons. First, sin separates us from God (v. 2). We first saw this when Adam and Eve were evicted from the Garden of Eden (Genesis 3:23-24). By the time of Isaiah, people were even more distant from God; they had lost the ability to experience his presence or communicate with him at all (Isaiah 59:2). Today, the distance has gotten so great that some people mistakenly think God is dead, or that he never existed at all.

Second, sin leads to a breakdown of fundamental values. The modern bumper sticker that reads "No justice. No peace." could just as easily have been written by Isaiah (v. 8). He mentions justice six times in this reading alone. But as we work for justice today, we must be careful not to define it according to a short list of political issues. Biblical justice means doing what's right for all people, especially the poor and oppressed (Psalm 82:3-4).

Finally, sin causes a rejection of truth. Isaiah used the image a person stumbling and lost in the street (Isaiah 59:14-15). Most people today believe in some form of their "own truth." But when truth becomes relative, society loses its reference points and wanders ever further from God.

It's no surprise that God is against sin. What is surprising is that in spite of our continual rebellion against him, God has had a plan to save us from it all along (vv. 20-21). The plan was to send a Redeemer (v. 20)—Jesus Christ—who could restore the broken relationship forever.

APPLY: In what ways do you need to demonstrate that you are against sin?

PRAY: Thank you, heavenly Father, that you've always had a plan for me to find forgiveness of my sin and a new relationship with you.

10 ❧ HO, HO, HO?

PRAY: Heavenly Father, you know how busy I am in my daily life. You also know how much I need to be still, be still, be still and know that you are God.

READ: Amos 5:1-27

REFLECT: Do you ever wonder how God feels when we sin? Perhaps he's like a shopping-mall Santa Claus. He doesn't really know what we've done, and he doesn't really care. He just chuckles and promises to give us what we want. Not exactly.

As we've discovered in this passage, God has some pretty strong things to say to folks who go through the motions of worship without acknowledging their sin. "I hate . . . I despise . . . I cannot stand . . . I will not accept . . . I will have no regard . . . I will not listen" (vv. 21-23). That's no shopping-mall Santa.

We might want to be more euphemistic about sin. "Well, nobody's perfect." Or "We all have our little peccadilloes." Or "That's just the way I am." But it's important not to gloss over the fact that God hates sin with a passion.

That's the message the prophet Amos had for the people of Israel in the eighth century B.C. They were piously attending worship and longing for the day when God would punish everyone else ("the day of the LORD" [v. 18]). But God was angry because these highly religious people weren't practicing what they preached. They abused the poor in order to live in luxury (v. 11); they manipulated the courts and deprived innocent people of justice (v. 12). In short, the society had become so corrupt that good people were afraid to speak out (v. 13). Some say that Amos could be describing Western society and the church today.

It can be frightening to think of God being so angry. But only when we understand the depth of his revulsion for sin can we fully appreciate the height of his love for us in sending his own Son. Jesus Christ willingly died for the sins of the world that God hated so much. That's not anger; it's overwhelming love.

APPLY: Amos encouraged his readers to seek the Lord (vv. 4, 6). How could you do that this week?

PRAY: Thank you, heavenly Father, that even though you know all about my sin, you loved me so much that you sent Jesus to deal with the consequences of it.

DISCUSSION QUESTIONS FOR "THE NEED FOR A SAVIOR"

1. How did you first become aware that there was such a thing as sin?

2. How do you define *sin* now?

3. Do you think the church and Christian people focus too much or not enough on sin? Why?

4. How does it make you feel to know that God *hates* sin? How does it make you feel that God solved the sin problem himself?

5. Do you think it's fair to say God has an "angry side"? Why?

6. Have you ever sensed a need for a Savior in your life? When and why?

7. Do you think it's possible to understand the good news about salvation without understanding the bad news about sin? Why or why not?

Previews of a Savior

IF YOU'VE EVER WATCHED TELEVISION OR been to a movie, you know what a preview is. It's a short promotion for a coming attraction. Usually the preview captures a quick taste of the most exciting parts of the full program or movie, and by the time you've seen several, you have a pretty good idea of what's coming.

In our next five readings we'll take a look at some fascinating previews of coming attractions found in the Bible. These are often referred to as "types." (Another kind of preview is found in the prophetic books, which we'll consider in future sections.) A biblical type is simply a person, thing or event in the Old Testament that points toward Jesus Christ in the New Testament. Many people find that a basic understanding of typology brings a new richness to their understanding of the Old Testament.

We must be careful, however, not to overdo our search for types. Some have tried to impose deep meaning on every detail in the Old Testament, and as a result they have come to some very speculative conclusions. This may be good for selling books, but it does not promote sound teaching. Even so, there is no need to "throw the baby out with the bathwater" since Jesus himself said that the Old Testament spoke about him (John 5:46).

To maintain our balance, we will consider five Old Testament types that are specifically referenced in the New Testament—the Passover, manna in the wilderness, Moses lifting up the serpent, the temple and

Jonah in the great fish. As you'll see, each one of these gives us a unique
picture of the Savior who would appear centuries later.

As we launch into our study of Old Testament types, we can be encouraged that we are following a teaching method that Jesus used with the two
disciples on the road to Emmaus, "And beginning with Moses and all the
Prophets, he [Jesus] explained to them what was said in all the Scriptures
concerning himself" (Luke 24:27).

11 ∾ SIGNIFICANT SYMBOLS

PRAY: Lord God, help me to understand you better as I read your Word
today.

READ: Exodus 12:1-30

REFLECT: Our passage today may seem a little gruesome—killing an-
imals, handling blood, sudden death—but in fact it is one of the most important passages in the Bible. The Passover represents a dramatic break-
through in the Old Testament; it's also a symbol of the most significant
event in the New Testament. Let's step back and get the context.

The Israelites had been slaves in Egypt for 430 years (Exodus 12:40-
41). In recent days Moses had challenged Pharaoh nine times with a
message from God, "Let my people go!" Each time it was accompanied
by a severe plague (Exodus 7:14—10:29). In this passage God un-
leashes the tenth and final plague—the death of the firstborn—and it
becomes the tipping point for the Israelites' exodus from Egypt (Exodus 12:31-42).

Our passage also contains two poignant connections to Jesus.

The first is the reference to a *lamb* (v. 3) that was sacrificed to avert
God's judgment (vv. 12-13). The writers of the New Testament often described Jesus as a lamb. John the Baptist called him "the Lamb of God"
(John 1:29). Peter referred to him as a "lamb without blemish" (1 Peter
1:19). And the apostle John described Jesus as the "Lamb who was slain"

(Revelation 5:12). The Passover lamb was one of the first great previews of God's plan of salvation.

A second connection to Jesus is the use of *blood*. Just as the blood of the Passover lamb became the essential element that saved the Israelites (vv. 7, 13), so the blood of Jesus shed on the cross was the essential element that secured salvation for all humankind. Jesus' death was the payment for sin. The New Testament has many references to this idea (Romans 5:9; Hebrews 9:11-14).

Jesus himself picked up on this theme at the Last Supper when he offered his followers a cup of wine and called it "the new covenant in my blood" (Luke 22:20). In so doing, he reengineered the Passover celebration to make his salvation available to all people (1 Corinthians 5:7).

APPLY: What does taking Communion symbolize for you? Is it a ritual or is it personal?

PRAY: "Just as I am, without one plea, / But that Thy blood was shed for me, / And that Thou bidst me come to Thee, / O Lamb of God I come, I come" (Charlotte Elliott, 1835).

12 ❧ TRUE BREAD

PRAY: Heavenly Father, you know there is so much on my mind today. But I just want to stop and thank you for the good things you've done in my life.

READ: Exodus 16:1-35

REFLECT: When I was growing up, our family went on some wonderful vacations together. But no matter how good the vacation had been, the journey home was always a challenge—being cooped up for a long time in a station wagon sometimes caused my three siblings and I to fuss and fight, much to my parents' frustration. That's exactly what happens in this passage.

God had miraculously taken the Israelites out of Egypt (Exodus 12:31-42) and through the Red Sea (Exodus 13:17—14:31). But the long journey through the desert caused them to have a family meltdown over food. Note that the word *grumble* is mentioned seven times in the first eleven verses of this chapter. No wonder Moses finally blew his stack (Exodus 16:20)! Even when we face a legitimate problem in our families, work places or churches, grumbling and complaining won't make things better.

God seems to look past the bickering of his people and again miraculously provides for them. First, he gets their attention with an awesome display of his glory (v. 10); then he delivers the food they were yelping for (vv. 13-15). It's encouraging that God uses the Israelites' moment of weakness as an opportunity to help them grow (v. 4). Thank God he doesn't wait for us to be perfect before he'll help us.

But embedded in this desert travelogue is another sign pointing to the Savior. In the New Testament, when the religious leaders demanded a miracle on demand, Jesus pointed to this passage in Exodus as his answer (John 6:25-59). First, he cleverly scolded his accusers to "stop grumbling" (John 6:43), a reference they would not have missed. But then he got to the main point: just as God provided manna to meet the physical need of people, so he, Jesus, was the "true bread" who satisfied the ultimate need of all people—the need for a restored and eternal relationship with God (John 6:48-51). That is Jesus' greatest miracle, and he offers it to you.

APPLY: Where are you today in your journey with Jesus?

PRAY: Forgive me, Lord, for the times I grumble about things in my life. Help me to focus on the big picture of the ways you've blessed me.

13 ∿ THE SNAKES

PRAY: "Open my eyes that I may see wonderful things in your law" (Psalm 119:18).

READ: Numbers 21:4-9

REFLECT: Alfred Hitchcock would have loved this passage. Like his classic movie *The Birds*, where humans are overrun by an ominous overpopulation of black birds, here the Israelites are overrun by an even scarier creature: snakes! It was God's judgment for the sin of his people. We should be careful not to incorrectly apply this passage. The main offense wasn't that the Israelites "went negative"; it was that they were challenging God (v. 5). That's the heart of all sin.

But this episode raises a tough question: does God cause natural disasters? The answer has two parts. First, because God created the world (Genesis 1:1) he has the power to cause or allow everything to happen. The Bible has many examples of this reality (Exodus 14:19-22; Matthew 8:27). But, second, we must ask, what is a disaster? Often God uses bad things for good purposes; in this case an infestation of snakes stopped the sinful behavior of his people. We may not be able to explain why some things happen in our world today, nor should we try to force a happy ending on every tragedy. Even so, we can be confident that nothing is outside God's loving purpose (Romans 8:28).

His main purpose is to provide a way for people to be saved. When the Israelites looked at the bronze replica, they were saved from the effects of the poison (vv. 8-9). Note that God didn't make the snakes go away (and he doesn't always make our problems go away). His miracle was to provide a way overcome them.

Jesus referred to this episode early in his ministry as a way of explaining his mission to a religious leader (John 3:14-15). Just as the bronze snake became the vehicle of the Israelites' salvation, so Jesus' death on the cross would be the vehicle for the salvation of all people who believe in him. How amazing that God used a complaining band of desert wanders to highlight his plan of salvation for the world.

APPLY: What do you complain about most? How can you tell the difference between "just complaining" and being angry at God?

PRAY: Lord, I don't understand some of the things that happen in my life. But I believe you are in control, so I ask you to open my eyes to what you are trying to teach me.

14 ∾ THE NEW TEMPLE

PRAY: Lord God, I worship you today. Help me to sense your presence as I read your Word and pray.

READ: 1 Kings 8:1-21

REFLECT: The people of Israel had finally made it. With their captivity in Egypt a distant memory, they now had their own land and their own king. Only one thing was missing: they didn't have a fitting place to worship the God of Abraham, Isaac and Jacob. But that's what makes this passage significant; it describes the "ribbon-cutting ceremony" for a magnificent new temple King Solomon built in Jerusalem.

The building was impressive in its architecture (1 Kings 6:1-38) and filled with extravagant furnishings (1 Kings 7:13-51). But its true significance is what would happen there: God's glory would be present (1 Kings 8:10-13). How mind-boggling that the Creator of the universe would be willing to take such a step! But that reveals something important about God: he wants to meet with his people.

Over the years, the temple was destroyed and rebuilt, and by the time of Jesus it stood at the center of Israel's religious, political and cultural identity. It had also become commercialized and out of touch with its original purpose, more like a strip mall than a place of worship.

It's no wonder that Jesus angrily cleaned house in the temple (John

2:12-17), or that the religious leaders then demanded proof of his authority. But the real issue was that he wanted everyone to know that this important Old Testament building had been pointing to him all along. "Destroy this temple," Jesus said, "and I will raise it again in three days" (John 2:19). Neither his opponents nor his disciples understood. But Jesus meant that as a result of his death and resurrection, *he* would replace Solomon's temple. Thereafter, meeting God would no longer be for the high priest behind a thick curtain (Matthew 27:51). It would be available to everyone who believes and follows Jesus.

APPLY: How could your church become more like a place to meet God and less like a shopping mall? When do you feel God's presence the most?

PRAY: Dear God, I'm hungry for a deeper experience of you. I focus my mind and heart on how awesome and loving you are.

15 ❧ RUNNING ON EMPTY

PRAY: Dear God, I believe that everything happens for a reason. And I'm so grateful that you know what it is.

READ: Jonah 1:1—4:11

REFLECT: Everyone knows the story of Jonah, but it's still a fun read. The man was called by God to preach a message of judgment to the wicked people in Nineveh, and he balked. Maybe Jonah was prejudiced against people outside his own community, or maybe he wanted to be popular instead of prophetic, or maybe he was just afraid of violent repercussions. Whatever his reason, Jonah foolishly tried to run from God. But that's no more foolish than when we think that we can engage in "secret sin." God always knows.

God also has a way of getting our secrets out into the open. One way is through our consciences (Jonah 1:10). The fact that we have a conscience at all is indirect proof that God exists. Where did our sense of right and wrong come from in the first place? Another way is by intervening in our circumstances; in Jonah's case, he was swallowed by a "great fish" (Jonah 1:17). That may never happen to you, but God will allow things in your life for a reason. That's why it's always good to ask, "Lord, what are you trying to say to me through this?"

Jesus clearly understood what God was saying through the experiences of Jonah (Matthew 12:38-45). When the skeptical religious leaders of his day asked for miraculous proof of his authenticity, Jesus referred to this Old Testament book. In essence he was saying the story of Jonah provided all the proof they needed. How? First, Jesus came to die. Just as Jonah was entombed in the great fish for three days, so Jesus would be in the tomb three days after his crucifixion. And second, Jesus would rise again. Just as the great fish gave up Jonah, so the grave would give up Jesus. The bottom line is, Jesus didn't come to impress people with magic tricks. He came to set them free from sin through his death and resurrection. And that's no fish story.

APPLY: Is there any area of your life in which you are running from God right now? Why? And what do you think you should do about it?

PRAY: Lord, you know I'm going through some tough things right now. I don't have all the answers, but I'm wondering what you are trying to say to me.

DISCUSSION QUESTIONS FOR "PREVIEWS OF A SAVIOR"

1. Which of the five Old Testament stories that we considered in this section taught you the most about Jesus Christ? Why?

2. Can you think of other familiar Old Testament passages that might give a picture of what happened in the New Testament?

3. How did this section affect your view of the Old Testament? of the Bible?

4. Can you think of some popular books, television programs or movies that seem to stray into speculative interpretations of the Bible? Where do they seem off track?

5. What do you think is the most effective way to respond to someone who seems to be misinterpreting the Bible? Correction, dialogue, tolerance . . . ?

6. For you, what are the most significant Christian symbols? Why?

7. In a postmodern society, which do you think is more effective in communicating Christian truth: symbols, examples, teaching, preaching or something else? Why?

Psalms About a Savior

THE BOOK OF PSALMS IS ONE OF THE MOST loved and perhaps most read sections in the entire Bible. It contains what amounts to the prayers, poems, praises and laments of some passionate servants of God from the past: people like David, Solomon, Moses, Asaph (the "worship leader" during David's lifetime) and several others.

Another feature that makes the psalms so rich in meaning is that they continue the developing story line about Jesus Christ that we've been following throughout the Bible. These psalms are often called "messianic psalms" because they contain previews of the coming Savior (see "Previews of a Savior" on pp. 35-36). Psalms that point to the Messiah are Psalms 2, 8, 16, 22, 24, 40, 41, 45, 69, 72, 89, 102, 110 and 118. (If you have the time, you may want to read all of these messianic psalms back to back to get the full effect.)

To give us a good sense of what these special psalms are all about, we will read five of the most popular ones; in so doing we'll gain several insights that instruct us today. First, we'll discover that Jesus often quoted from the psalms, which reminds us that when we read the Old Testament, we're reading the same Bible Jesus read. And what's obvious is that Jesus studied and memorized the Scriptures; that's a good example for us.

Second, we'll discover that these psalms give us an amazingly graphic picture of what would happen to Jesus. (We'll see this dynamic again in the prophetic books.) One of the most famous messianic psalms is Psalm 22, the one Jesus quoted on the cross, "My God, my God, why have you forsaken me?" But what's even more striking is the detailed description of a crucifixion that it contains, which reminds us that the cross was no accident. God knew all along how he planned to offer salvation to the world, and to us.

So get ready to dig into the psalms about a Savior.

16 ∾ THE CASE FOR CHRIST

PRAY: Heavenly Father, I'd like to have a closer relationship with you today, as close as a child feels toward a loving parent.

READ: Psalm 2:1-12

REFLECT: From 1945 to 1991, the Soviet Union was one of two superpowers in the world. Yet in spite of a strong central government and a feared military capability, the U.S.S.R. had a fatal flaw: it rejected God. Atheism was its official policy, and Christianity was brutally suppressed. In the end it wasn't a nuclear confrontation that toppled the mighty communist regime. Rather, it was undone by the faithful witness and courageous resistance of the church.

That would come as no surprise to the writer of this psalm, whose intent was to advise the kings of Israel on the key to successful leadership. Foolish kings "conspire" and "plot" to banish God from his earth (vv. 1-3). Laughable as that may seem, especially to God (v. 4), it still happens today. Increasingly, Western democracies are forgetting that their ultimate authority is God, not the majority. Regardless of the political system, any nation that forgets God is headed for trouble. Wise kings, on the other hand, serve the Lord (v. 11) and reap the benefits of doing so for themselves and their people (vv. 8-9).

But there's more to this psalm than meets the eye. Viewed from the perspective of the New Testament we see several phrases that point to Jesus.

The psalm's description of a Father's approval of his Son (v. 7) echoes what God would later say to Jesus (Matthew 3:17; Luke 9:35). And the name given to Jesus, Messiah, means "Anointed One," the very phrase used in this psalm (v. 2). And when the apostles Peter and John were being persecuted for speaking about Jesus after his resurrection and ascension, they quoted this psalm (Acts 4:23-31). Put it all together and we realize that centuries before Jesus appeared, the Holy Spirit was already developing a case for Christ.

APPLY: In what ways do countries reject God today? What are some effective and ineffective ways leaders attempt to bring God into politics? Should God be part of the political process?

PRAY: Lord Jesus, regardless of what others do, I desire to follow you. Help me to influence others in your direction today.

17 ∾ AT THE CROSS

PRAY: Dear God, I'm hungry for a deeper understanding of your love for me today.

READ: Psalm 22:1-31

REFLECT: It's not difficult to see how this psalm relates to Jesus; it's a vivid description of what Jesus would experience at his crucifixion. In fact, it was this very psalm that Jesus quoted while he hung on the cross: "My God, my God, why have you forsaken me?" (Psalm 22:1; Mark 15:34). No doubt Jesus memorized these words as he grew up. Memorizing especially meaningful Bible verses may seem like an esoteric spiritual discipline, but it can become a reservoir of spiritual strength in times of trial (Psalm 119:11).

But to fully appreciate Psalm 22, we need to consider what it meant in its original context. Written by David, the psalm describes the inner feelings of a man in trouble, big trouble. Have you ever faced a problem so great, so devastating, that it affected your attitude, your activities, your health and everything in your world? That's what David is feeling here. One of David's great strengths was his ability to communicate his feelings.

Another was his reflex for turning to God first when the chips were down. He did this by forcing himself to remember what God had done in the past (v. 4); that gave him hope and enabled him to trust. He also took time out for praising (v. 25) and worshiping God (v. 29) in the middle of the crisis. That's how David weathered the storms in his life and what made him a "man after [God's] own heart" (Acts 13:22).

This psalm also causes us to admire the unique nature of the Bible. How could it be that nearly one thousand years before Jesus lived, David could describe the specific details of the way Jesus would die (Psalm 22:16; John 19:24-29), or what would happen at the foot of the cross (Psalm 22:18; John 19:24-25) or even what Jesus' enemies would say (Psalm 22:8; Matthew 27:41-43)? The only answer can be that it was God who inspired David to write what he did (2 Timothy 3:16; 2 Peter 1:21). The Bible is God's book, and Jesus is the main character from start to finish.

APPLY: How do you react when the bottom drops out of your world? How has God come to your aid in past times of trouble?

PRAY: Lord Jesus, it's hard for me to imagine what you went through on the cross. All I can say is thank you, thank you, thank you!

18 ❧ DEEP WATERS

PRAY: Heavenly Father, please give me a deeper sense of your presence and your priorities as I read your word today.

READ: Psalm 69:1-36

REFLECT: The psalms have always been the most meaningful to me when I am in trouble. I remember once being part of a financial collapse in a ministry that was so overwhelming I thought I'd never get out. On the outside, I was going through the motions of my normal life. But inside, all I could think about was the looming crisis. In my desperation, I read the psalms over and over; it was enormously helpful to read the heart cries of people who had nowhere else to turn but God.

That's what's happening in this Psalm 69. David is in "deep waters" (vv. 2, 14) and is calling out for God's help. It's not clear what particular problem David faced. But it is clear that "the man after [God's] own heart" (Acts 13:22) had gotten himself into "a big old jam." God doesn't help us because we are perfect. He helps us because in our desperation we turn to him.

Note how David responded to his overwhelming problem. First, he honestly described the situation to God (Psalm 69:1-4). Next, he examined his own heart first, instead of pointing fingers at others (vv. 5-6). Sometimes God uses a crisis to expose the sins we've been unable or unwilling to confess to him. Finally, David makes his request known to God (vv. 13-18) and takes time to praise God (vv. 30-36).

This psalm was especially meaningful to Jesus; he quoted it when explaining why the world hated him and his followers (John 15:25), and no doubt saw his own suffering on the cross echoed in the statement "they persecute those you wound" (Psalm 69:26). And it turns out that the references to gall and vinegar (v. 21) are prophetic of the details of Jesus' death (Matthew 27:34, 45). The disciples too were familiar with this psalm, seeing it as an explanation for Jesus' clearing of the temple (John 2:17).

Take a minute to read these verses one more time and marvel at how they've spoken so poignantly to struggling people down through the ages, whether they be David, Jesus, the disciples, me or you.

APPLY: What's the biggest crisis you face at the moment? What do you think God might be trying to say to you through it?

PRAY: Lord, I'm so thankful that I don't have to be perfect for you to

help me or to love me. Forgive me for not turning to you first when I get
in a jam.

19 ∾ WHO'S TALKING?

PRAY: Lord, I ask that you would transform my discipline of reading the
Bible into a time of meeting and hearing you.

READ: Psalm 110:1-7

REFLECT: I've always found Psalm 110 to be confusing. Who's doing
the talking? It seems as if there are two "Lords" (v. 1). And what's the main
point? It seems like a jumble of biblical allusions. Yet the New Testament
refers to this psalm more than any other. What's so important about these
seven verses?

The first thing to notice is the psalm is built around two direct statements from God (vv. 1, 4); what follows each is David's commentary on
what God has said. Next, it helps to consider what this psalm meant to its
original hearers. Over the years it would have been recited to honor the
royal descendents of King David at various special occasions. From that
perspective the first section (vv. 1-3) is an affirmation of the king's power.
God ("the LORD") is inviting the king ("my Lord") to sit next to him. The
second section (vv. 4-7) is an affirmation of the king's unique spiritual
leadership. Melchizedek (v. 4) was both king of Jerusalem and the "priest
of God Most High" who blessed Abraham (Genesis 14:18-20).

But the most significant thing about this psalm is the way it points to
the coming Messiah. Jesus affirmed this when he quoted these verses to
challenge the religious leaders who doubted he was the Son of God (Matthew 22:41-45). They thought the Messiah would be merely a human de-
scendant of David. But Jesus demonstrated, by referring to Psalm 110,
that the Messiah would also be the divine Son of God. He then applied all
of that symbolism to himself. In other words, Jesus was saying he was the
Messiah, the human-divine Savior of the world. The apostle Peter empha-

sized this point in his Pentecost sermon (Acts 2:29-36), as did the writer of Hebrews (Hebrews 5:6; 7:1-28).

Once we sort through the complexity of this short psalm, we are left with a simple fact: Jesus is the Son of God. And that's the essential message of the entire Bible.

APPLY: For you, what are the most convincing proofs that Jesus was who he said he was, the Son of God and Savior of the world?

PRAY: Lord Jesus, there are many things about you I don't fully understand. But I know enough to believe that you love me, and I thank you for that.

20 ❧ TRY TO REMEMBER

PRAY: Lord, I've got a million things swirling in my mind right now. But the thing I want most is to know and experience more of you.

READ: Psalm 118:1-29

REFLECT: Psalm 118 contains one of "the greatest hits" from the book of Psalms: "This is the day the LORD has made; let us rejoice and be glad in it" (v. 24) has become the opening sentence for countless worship services around the world.

Originally the psalm commemorated an unspecified victory in Israel's history. Apparently the people had faced a back-against-the-wall situation from which God had miraculously delivered them (vv. 5-13). That produced this unrestrained expression of joy and praise to God (vv. 14-28). When are you the most enthusiastic about praising God? People who have most recently experienced God's help are often the most energetic about praising him. That's why it's important to remember what God has done for us. It keeps our faith joyful and alive.

In the middle of this celebration of God's past deliverance, however, are two references to an even greater deliverance he planned in the future.

"The stone the builders rejected has become the capstone" (v. 22). Jesus quoted this verse at the end of his parable about the evil tenants (Matthew 21:33-46). His point? That he, Jesus, was he stone the religious leaders had rejected but whom God would make into the cornerstone (capstone) of his church. Peter expanded on this theme after the resurrection, calling Jesus "the living Stone" (1 Peter 2:4-7).

"Blessed is he who comes in the name of the LORD" (v. 26). This is one of the phrases shouted by the crowds during Jesus' triumphal entry into Jerusalem one week prior to his death on the cross (Matthew 21:1-11).

The greater deliverance God had in mind was his plan to save the world from sin and to offer people a way to have a relationship with him. That was accomplished on the cross, the event we commemorate by taking Communion. How joyful are you when you receive the bread and the cup?

APPLY: Have you ever faced a back-against-the-wall situation from which God delivered you? What happened? How does that help you praise God today?

PRAY: Take a few minutes to joyfully thank God for the ways he's helped and delivered you in your life.

DISCUSSION QUESTIONS FOR "PSALMS ABOUT A SAVIOR"

1. Which of the five psalms in this section communicated the most to you about Jesus Christ? Why?

2. How would you respond to a friend who said, "The psalms describe the struggles of someone long ago, but any comparison to Jesus is purely coincidence"?

3. Why do you think Jesus read and memorized Scripture? Can you think of other times when his biblical knowledge helped him or came into play?

4. What motivates you the most to read the Bible? When has the Bible meant the most to you in your life? Why?

5. What do you find are the biggest obstacles to reading the Bible regularly? How could you overcome them?

6. Have you ever tried to memorize a verse or passage of Scripture? How did it go? (Can you recite a favorite verse or passage now?)

7. Many people find that the Bible becomes more meaningful when they are in a crisis. Why do you suppose that is so? Has this ever been your experience?

Prophecies About a Savior

WHEN YOU THINK ABOUT PROPHECY, what comes to mind? Perhaps you think of an exciting movie where the protagonist unwittingly stumbles into a perplexing set of events that trace back to some weird and ancient prophecy. Or maybe you think of a roadside psychic whose sign claims she can tell you about your future in love, business and life (for a mere five dollars). Or maybe you think of a religious extremist who predicts the end of the world in a new book and speaking tour.

Whatever you think about prophecy, it's important to understand that the Bible takes it very seriously and contains lots of it. In fact, there are seventeen prophetic books in the Old Testament; five longer ones (the "major" prophets, Isaiah through Daniel) and twelve shorter ones (the "minor" prophet, Hosea through Malachi).

So what exactly is biblical prophecy? At its heart, it's about proclaiming God's truth in a particular situation (*forth*-telling). Over the years God's people (the Israelites) developed some very sinful habits, like idolatry, corruption and oppressing the poor. The prophets forcefully articulated what God's standards were and how he wanted his people to live.

Another aspect of biblical prophecy involves predicting God's plan for the future (*fore*telling). In the Old Testament one of the most common themes of the prophetic books was a coming day of judgment, "the day of the Lord." Many of the prophets warned God's people that their idolatry and sin would eventually bring punishment. These prophecies all came true when Babylon destroyed Jerusalem and took God's people into exile in 586 B.C.

Of course the most important feature of biblical prophecy is that whether it involved forth-telling or foretelling, it was not just the words and thoughts of a man. As the apostle Peter said, "For prophecy never had its origin in the will of man, but men spoke from God as they were carried along by the Holy Spirit" (2 Peter 1:21). A prophet was someone who spoke for God.

But there's another important feature of Old Testament prophecy that will be the focus of our next five readings—it frequently predicted the coming of the Messiah, who would bring God's salvation to earth. We'll start by examining the first hint we get of this theme in the book of Genesis. We'll then read a few of the hundreds of specific predictions about this Anointed One scattered throughout the prophetic books. By the time we complete this section, there will be no mystery—Jesus Christ perfectly fulfilled every prophecy about the coming Messiah.

21 ✧ CHOSEN PEOPLE

PRAY: Heavenly Father, I ask that you make my mind sharp and my heart open as I look into your Word today.

READ: Genesis 12:1-9

REFLECT: The Bible got off to a great start; God created a perfect world, and Adam and Eve had a perfect life. But sin changed all that. Human beings quickly found themselves separated from God and trapped in a wicked world spiraling out of control (Genesis 6:5). Sounds like today. But that's what makes Genesis 12:1-9 so significant; it marks a new beginning in God's dealings with humankind.

We don't get much background on Abram. All we know is that when he was seventy-five years old (v. 4), God told him to "leave" everything and "go" to an unknown land (v. 1). Regardless of your age, could you let go of everything to follow God's call? It was this willingness to abandon himself to God that made Abram one of the greatest examples of faith in the entire Bible (Genesis 15:6).

But the call of Abram was no random act of unkindness. God was putting in motion an incredible plan to reverse the effects of sin and to give humans a way to have close fellowship with him once again. At this point God only gives a short summary of what he had in mind (Genesis 12:2-3). It would take thousands of years for his plan of salvation to fully unfold.

The plan had two major components. The first was to create "a great nation" (v. 2) from Abram's family, who would eventually become the Israelites. It was to these people that God uniquely revealed himself over the centuries. He did it through a variety of incredible experiences and miracles, and eventually through the Ten Commandments and the law. Through it all, the people began to understand who God was and how he wanted them to live. The second part of the plan was to "bless . . . all peoples on earth" (v. 3) through his chosen people. It would take thousands of years and a lot of pain and suffering, but the great blessing was Jesus Christ, the Savior of the world.

At this point, Abram had no idea what God had in mind. All he knew was that God said "go," and so he did. It's amazing what God can accomplish through one person who is willing to trust and obey him.

APPLY: What things hold you back from wholeheartedly following God? In what area of your life do you feel God is asking you to trust him more?

PRAY: Lord, I don't want to follow you out of a sense of guilt or duty. But I do want to develop a greater trust in you and your purposes for me.

22 ◦ THE GOOD SHEPHERD

PRAY: Lord, there are so many problems in the world, and even in my life. But no matter what, I can always praise you for how good and great and loving you are.

READ: Jeremiah 23:1-9

REFLECT: After God announced his plan to bless all nations of the world through his chosen people (Genesis 12:2-3), it would be nice to think they lived happily ever after. But as we see in the rest of the Bible, it didn't work out that way. The Israelites just couldn't resist the temptation to do things their way instead of God's (that's the short definition of sin), and it got them into all kinds of trouble.

Jeremiah was one of the prophets God sent to denounce Israel's sin and turn them back to God. It wasn't a job he really wanted (Jeremiah 1:4-19), and it caused him a lot of grief (Jeremiah 20:1-18). But Jeremiah faithfully expressed God's perspective to the people around him. That's still difficult to do today, but our world desperately needs men and women who will speak "the truth in love" (Ephesians 4:15) in spite of the consequences.

One group who especially felt the heat of Jeremiah's prophecy was the religious leaders ("shepherds," Jeremiah 23:1-2). We know from other parts of this book that they were following a path of idolatry, injustice and immorality instead of truly caring for the people (v. 2). In response, God says he's going to defrock the religious leaders and take the reigns himself ("I myself . . ." v. 3). That should be a wake-up call to the leaders of God's people in any age.

It also opens the door for another prophesy about God's plan. Jeremiah tells us that the Savior God was preparing to send would not only be a descendent of David but also something more—"a righteous Branch" (v. 5) and "The LORD Our Righteousness" (v. 6). In other words, God himself was planning to step into the picture to reestablish the right relationship between us and him that sin had destroyed. The way he would do that is by sending his own Son, Jesus Christ (1 Corinthians 1:30). Viewed from our perspective, the tragic impact of these bad shepherds has a good purpose in God's plan; they highlighted the need for the good Shepherd (John 10:11-18).

APPLY: Is there a situation in your life where you sense God "nudging you" to speak out for him? How could you do this?

PRAY: Jesus, help me to see the difference between *my* way and *your* way of doing things in some of the difficult areas of my life.

23 ✢ O LITTLE TOWN OF BETHLEHEM

PRAY: "Praise the LORD, O my soul; all my inmost being, praise his holy name" (Psalm 103:1).

READ: Micah 5:1-5

REFLECT: Micah was no TV preacher. His messages weren't slick, packaged or positive. They were rough, passionate and hard-hitting (for example, Micah 3:1-4). And he would have been a terrible fundraiser because his main theme was to denounce sin, especially of the wealthy and powerful. "Come on, boss. You'll never build a donor base like that!" But Micah wasn't trying to be popular; he was trying to be faithful to the message he had been given (Micah 1:1): God was going to punish Israel for her sins. Micah's prophecy was fulfilled when Babylon destroyed Jerusalem and took the people into captivity.

Buried in the middle of his challenging prophetic book, however, we find our passage today, which is one of the most unique in the Old Testament. In it Micah looks beyond his current situation to a time far in the future when God would send a Savior whose rule would extend to "the ends of the earth" (Micah 5:4). Even in just these few verses we learn several important details about this coming Savior, all of which were fulfilled by Jesus Christ.

His origins. The Savior would come from the little town of Bethlehem

(v. 2). At the time of Jesus' birth, this was the commonly held understanding (Matthew 2:3-6). It was such an unlikely place, and yet God orchestrated an incredible chain of events—a census of the Roman empire, a late-night trip by a pregnant woman and her fiancé, and a birth in a stable—to make it happen (Luke 2:1-7). Jesus fulfilled this very specific prophecy made centuries before his birth.

His character. Micah picks up on the shepherd imagery, as have other prophets. But he adds that the Savior's strength and majesty won't be based on human ability but rather on "the name of the LORD his God" (Micah 5:4). And the Savior won't just achieve a time of peace, "he will be their peace" (v. 5). Micah was prophesying about none other than Jesus Christ, who made peace with God by his death on the cross.

APPLY: Do you feel like you are at peace with God? Why?

PRAY: Heavenly Father, I marvel at the intricate nature of our plan of salvation and that you have given me the opportunity to understand it.

24 ～ THE HUMBLE KING

PRAY: Heavenly Father, here are all the things that are worrying me now . . . I need your help to quiet my mind and heart so I can hear what you want to say to me.

READ: Zechariah 9:9-17

REFLECT: Many Old Testament prophets warned of a coming day of judgment, which finally arrived with the fall of Jerusalem and Israel's exile into Babylon in 586 B.C. Zechariah lived after these terrible events at a time when the Israelites had been allowed to return to their land. In the first part of his prophesy Zechariah encourages the people to continue rebuilding the temple and to avoid falling into the sin patterns of the past (Zechariah 1—8). In the second part he looks forward to the coming of a very special king (Zechariah 9—14). The question is, what kind of king would he be?

After living in captivity for over seventy years, it would be natural for the Israelites to want a strong king, someone who would fight fire with fire. But revenge and violence only make things worse, as the history of the Middle East and our own relationships clearly prove. The king Zechariah described was far different than anything Israel had seen or experienced. First, he would be humble (Zechariah 9:9), not proud or arrogant. Second, he would establish genuine peace throughout the world (v. 10), not just the protection of Israel. And finally, he would institute a new kind of freedom, one based on "the blood of my covenant with you" (v. 11).

It's not hard to see how these prophesies were fulfilled, starting about five centuries later. Jesus was *humble*—he entered Jerusalem riding on a donkey (Matthew 21:1-11); he was the epitome of a servant leader (John 13:1-17). Jesus brought *freedom*—by dying on the cross, he freed people from the prison of sin and enabled them to have a relationship with God once again (Ephesians 1:7). Jesus will bring *peace*—someday in the future Jesus will come again to establish an everlasting peace for those who believe in him (1 Thessalonians 4:16-17).

When we put all these pieces together, the picture becomes clear: Jesus Christ *was* and *is* the Savior King that God promised through Zechariah so many years ago.

APPLY: Have you ever tried to get revenge on someone who wronged you? What did you learn? How could you demonstrate the kind of humility Jesus had?

PRAY: Spend some time praying for the people who have wronged you most recently.

25 ∿ FUTURE CLUES

PRAY: Lord God, please enable me to hear your voice as I read and reflect on this passage today.

READ: Zechariah 12:1—13:9

REFLECT: How do Bible books like Zechariah, or any of the Old Testament prophets, relate to life today? After all, they describe ancient times that are completely unfamiliar to us now. (Plus they have weird names!)

The answer is simple: They show us what God is like. By reading how he reacted to particular situations in the past, we learn how he wants us to live today. In addition, the prophetic books often contain clues or references to more significant events in the future.

That's what we find in our passage today. It describes a time when Jerusalem would be surrounded and outnumbered by her enemies (Zechariah 12:2-3), sadly, a situation that has occurred often throughout history. But Israel will prevail, Zechariah says, not because of her own power and might, but rather "because the LORD Almighty is their God" (v. 5). That's still true for us today; the ultimate source of our safety and success is not our own strength and abilities. Rather it's God's work on our behalf, which is why praise is so appropriate and pride so outrageous.

Our passage also contains several of the "future clues" that make the prophetic books so relevant. One is Zechariah's reference to "the one they have pierced" (v. 10). In his Gospel account, John linked this verse to Jesus' death on the cross (John 19:36-37). It was the event that provided the cleansing from sin that Zechariah anticipated (Zechariah 13:1). Another "future clue" is found in the poem about the shepherd and the sheep (Zechariah 13:7-9), a familiar biblical theme, as we've seen. Jesus quoted this very passage to predict how Peter and the rest of the disciples would desert him at his arrest (Matthew 26:31-35).

But there's one other thing that makes the ancient prophetic books come alive today: they often quote God directly ("This is the word of the LORD," Zechariah 12:1). God spoke to the prophets, and they wrote it down (that's what an "oracle" is). And when God speaks, we'd better listen.

APPLY: Is pride always bad? How could you avoid becoming proud in ways you shouldn't? How could you make praise for God a bigger part of your day?

PRAY: Dear God, thank you that you are a God who has spoken in the past and who continues to speak today. Help me to be a doer of your word and not a hearer only (James 1:22-25).

DISCUSSION QUESTIONS FOR "PROPHECIES ABOUT A SAVIOR"

1. How do you see the theme of prophecy portrayed in popular culture today?

2. What is your view of prophecy? How would you describe it in your own words?

3. Do you think people today make too much or too little of biblical prophecy? Why, and does it make a difference?

4. How can you be sure your understanding of prophecy is correct?

5. Do you think there is one correct interpretation of the Bible? How should you relate to people who have a different understanding of the Bible than you?

6. For you, which of the prophecies in this section is the most significant proof that Jesus was the Messiah? Why?

7. Do you think there are any genuine prophets in the world today—people who are *forth*-tellers or *fore*tellers on behalf of God? Who are they, and why do you think so?

More Prophecies About a Savior

WHEN IT COMES TO THE OLD TESTAMENT PROPHETS, Isaiah is "the big man on campus." For one thing, he was active for somewhere between forty to sixty years, and his ministry outlasted four kings. And his book is the longest of all the prophets—sixty-six chapters in all—and is the most-quoted prophetic book in the New Testament. But the most significant thing about Isaiah is that his prophecy gives us the most information about the coming Messiah, which is why we'll spend the next five readings pursuing what the Lord said through him.

The clearest descriptions of the Messiah are found in four so-called Servant Songs, which we find in the book of Isaiah. (They are Isaiah 42:1-9; 49:1-6; 50:4-9; 52:13—53:12.) They all describe various aspects of "the servant of the Lord." Who exactly is this servant? Scholars love to debate questions like that, but for our purposes we can boil it down to this: the phrase refers both to the nation of Israel *and* the coming Messiah.

If you look ahead to the New Testament, you'll see that Jesus took the servant-of-the-Lord mantle onto himself at the beginning of his ministry by quoting from one of the Servant Songs.

The scroll of the prophet Isaiah was handed to him. Unrolling it, he found the place where it is written:

"The Spirit of the Lord is on me,
    because he has anointed me

> to preach good news to the poor.
> He has sent me to proclaim freedom for the prisoners
> and recovery of sight for the blind,
> to release the oppressed,
> to proclaim the year of the Lord's favor."

Then he rolled up the scroll, gave it back to the attendant and sat down. The eyes of everyone in the synagogue were fastened on him, and he began by saying to them, "Today this scripture is fulfilled in your hearing." (Luke 4:17-21)

Jesus was keenly aware that Isaiah had prophesied about him; it was a fact that guided his ministry on earth.

But perhaps the most famous passage in the book of Isaiah is the one that describes the "suffering servant" (52:13—53:12). God inspired Isaiah to describe the crucifixion of Jesus in graphic detail long before it happened. And when Jesus walked the earth, he frequently explained that his mission was to suffer (Matthew 16:21). And yet no one understood—not the crowds, not the religious leaders and not even his own disciples. It's hard to imagine that the God of the universe would send his own Son to die for the sins of humankind, but that's exactly what he did. And that's exactly what Isaiah prophesied—*almost eight hundred years before it happened!*

26 ❧ GOD WITH US

PRAY: Heavenly Father, my heart's desire is to experience your presence in a fresh new way today.

READ: Isaiah 7:1-25

REFLECT: Isaiah 7:1-25 contains one of the most well-known and debated prophecies about the coming Messiah in the entire Old Testament. Isaiah says that a virgin will give birth to a son who will be called Immanuel, which literally means "God with us" (v. 14). The New Testament makes clear this prophecy was fulfilled in the birth of Jesus Christ (Matthew 1:18-25). But to fully understand these verses, we need to consider what they meant to the original hearers.

Since 925 B.C., God's chosen people had been split into two rival kingdoms, Judah in the south (the tribes of Judah and Benjamin), and Israel in the north (the remaining ten tribes). At the beginning of Isaiah 7 we learn that Pekah, the king of Israel, and Rezin, the king of Aram (Syria), are attacking King Ahaz in Jerusalem, the capital of the southern kingdom. God's message is reassuring, saying in essence, "Stay calm. I will deal with Pekah and Rezin" (vv. 3-9).

When we find ourselves facing political battles today—whether at work, in the community or even in the church—we need to remember that ultimately success is dependent on God, not on our cleverness or political skill (v. 9). For many years I worked with Chuck Colson at a ministry called Prison Fellowship. On his desk was a plaque that said, "Faithfulness, not success."

Trusting God when the pressure is on can be tough. Even when Ahaz was offered a confirming sign, he hesitated (vv. 10-12) because he wanted to form his own alliance with Assyria. God gave the sign anyway: the birth of a Son named Immanuel. For the original hearers, this probably meant that when God delivered Judah from the attacks of Pekah and Rezin, young mothers would name their sons in memory of God's deliverance, just as Isaiah had named his son after a future deliverance of God (Shear-Jashub [v. 3] literally means "a remnant will return").

But the sign also predicted God's greatest deliverance, sending his own Son, Jesus Christ, to deliver all people from sin. The great miracle is that because of Jesus' entry into human history, God is with us forever.

APPLY: Are you facing any situations of "political pressure" at work, in the community or in your church? How could you be more faithful to God in the midst of the pressure?

PRAY: Ask God to help you remain faithful to him in the midst of the pressures and struggles you face today.

27 ❧ HOPE FOR THE FUTURE

PRAY: Lord, I ask that you would renew my sense of true joy as I spend time with you today.

READ: Isaiah 9:1-8

REFLECT: In these verses Isaiah gives God's people a message of hope. They sure needed it. As we discovered in Isaiah 7, Jerusalem was being attacked by two armies. God delivered his people from that threat only to allow an even bigger one; the powerful nation of Assyria would soon attack as punishment for their sin (Isaiah 7:17; 8:6-8).

It's natural to want God to solve the problems we find ourselves in. He can and often does. But what he really cares about is helping us understand how to have a right relationship with him. Sometimes that means he allows us to go through trials to strengthen our faith. Sometimes it means he allows painful experiences to expose our hidden sins. But all the time he is at work for our good (Romans 8:28).

That's why the word *nevertheless* is such a hopeful start to Isaiah 9. In spite of Judah's sin, and in spite of all its troubles, God was planning something good in the future. Not only would he take away their gloom and distress (v. 1) but he was also planning a future that would be wonderful in at least three ways:

- *Light.* God would turn the darkness into light (v. 2). In other words, he was promising an eventual deliverance from the Assyrian invasion.

- *Joy.* This deliverance would lead to unrestrained joy (v. 3). When God intervenes to solve our problems, it's hard not to praise him with abandon.

- *The coming Messiah.* Finally, this vision of the future would culminate in the birth of a child who would become a unique leader (vv. 6-7), the promised Messiah. This prophecy was fulfilled in Jesus Christ, who delivered us from the darkness of sin and established an everlasting kingdom for those who put their trust in him.

The source of hope is not the absence of problems, as the people of God have discovered throughout the ages. Rather, it is knowing that God is there and in control no matter what happens.

APPLY: How has God used the circumstances of your life to draw you to himself?

PRAY: Heavenly Father, in spite of how things appear at times, I'm so thankful that you are in charge of this world and of my life.

28 ∾ CHOSEN SERVANT

PRAY: Spend some time confessing your sins to God and then thanking him for his forgiveness.

READ: Isaiah 42:1-9

REFLECT: Our reading today is the first of the four "Servant Songs" that we find throughout the book of Isaiah (see "More Prophecies About a Savior," pp. 62-63). At the time Isaiah uttered this prophesy, no doubt he was thinking of the nation of Israel. But God used Isaiah's words to also communicate something about the coming Messiah. So what do we learn about this unique servant?

He has been chosen by God (v. 1). Israel had been chosen by God long ago when God promised to make Abram's family into a "great nation" (Genesis 12:2). Isaiah prophesied that one day a Savior would come who would be uniquely chosen by God.

He is God's instrument of salvation (v. 6). From the very birth of the chosen people, God's intent was to bring blessing to all people through them (Genesis 12:3). Isaiah builds on that theme and says that the servant would be filled with the Spirit of God and would establish justice for all, including the weak and downtrodden (the "bruised reeds" and "smoldering wicks" [Isaiah 42:3]).

At his baptism, Jesus was filled with the Holy Spirit (Matthew 3:16); by his death and resurrection he provided the way of salvation for all people. Jesus himself said that he was the fulfillment of this passage (Matthew 12:15-21). When the Pharisees were plotting to kill him, Jesus took his disciples aside and used this passage to explain who he was—God's promised Messiah.

Woven through the Old Testament is the story of the Savior God planned to send, the one who would save people from their sin and give them a real relationship with the living God. By the time we get to the New Testament, we'll learn that the Savior was none other than Jesus Christ. The more you read the Bible, the more you discover that the Bible is "his story."

APPLY: Who are the weak and downtrodden—the "bruised reeds" and "smoldering wicks"—in your world? How could you be God's instrument of justice for them?

PRAY: Lord God, there are so many areas of injustice in this world. I ask that you would give me the courage and conviction to work for justice in one situation in the days ahead.

29 ✎ MAN OF SORROWS

PRAY: Heavenly Father, please give me a deeper understanding of what your Son went through for me.

READ: Isaiah 52:13—53:12

REFLECT: In this well-known passage Isaiah introduces us to the "suffering servant" and in the process gives us a detailed picture of what Jesus would experience on the cross. What's amazing is that Isaiah wrote these verses about eight hundred years before Jesus lived! This highlights the unique nature of the Bible; it is inspired by God (2 Timothy 3:16).

The odd thing is that the people closest to Jesus, his disciples, missed the point of this passage. They wanted a conquering hero, not a suffering servant. It's easy to make the same mistake today. We assume God will work through the power structures of our day, so we spend a lot of time and energy trying to influence them. But the truth is, God often prefers to use the weak and the lowly to accomplish his purposes in the world (Luke 1:46-55).

So what details about this unique servant did the Holy Spirit reveal to Isaiah? The first and most obvious is that *he would have to suffer* (Isaiah 53:3, 7, 10). It's interesting that it was the "LORD's will to crush him and cause him to suffer" (v. 10). Sometimes God allows bad things to happen to good people, not because he's mean or enjoys watching people squirm. Rather, he knows that the hard road is often the only way to change our hearts and lives for the better.

The second detail is that *the servant's suffering would pay for the sins of others* (Isaiah 53:5-6, 12). That's the key to this passage, and it's exactly what Jesus did on the cross. Finally, Isaiah predicts that the *suffering servant would eventually be restored and glorified* (Isaiah 53:11-12), which is what happened when God brought Jesus back to life in his resurrection.

Isaiah couldn't have understood the full implications of what he prophesied, and it took a while for the apostles to figure it out (1 Peter 2:21-25). But we now have the great advantage of seeing the full picture of God's plan of salvation. The challenge for us is how do we respond?

APPLY: Why do you think God often chooses to use the weak and lowly to do his work?

PRAY: Spend some time prayerfully responding to what Jesus did on the cross. You might want to admit your questions and doubts, or for the first time say, "Yes I believe," or from the depths of your heart thank Jesus for saving you.

30 ~ MISSION STATEMENT

PRAY: Lord, I sometimes think too much about the glass being half empty. I pray that you would open my eyes to the good things you are doing in my life and the world today.

READ: Isaiah 61:1-11

REFLECT: It's about time for some good news! After all the gloom, doom and suffering described by the prophets so far, it's nice to read about freedom, comfort and a time of "the LORD's favor" (v. 2). Ah—now that feels better.

But this is much more than a feel-good passage; it gives us a vision for the restoration of God's people. The really good news in these verses is that God never abandons his people. As we've discovered, the Israelites had been attacked and taken captive by powerful nations around them. Their key city and temple had been destroyed. And all of it happened because they had sinned against God. But here, Isaiah describes a time when everything would be put right and the Israelites' despair would be turned to praise (v. 3).

This underscores two aspects of God's character. First, he is a God of *hope*. Regardless of what we've done, and regardless of what messes we make of our lives, with God we can have a fresh start and a new future. That doesn't mean all our trials will magically go away; some problems take years to be resolved, some never completely disappear. But even so, God is always at work for our ultimate good (Jeremiah 29:11-13; Romans 8:28), as he was for the Israelites. A second aspect of God's character is that he passionately *loves justice* and *hates sin* (v. 8). The surest way to experience God's blessing is to be passionate about his priorities.

This passage had special significance for Jesus; he used it as the mission statement for his life on earth. Near the beginning of his public ministry, Jesus stood and read this passage in the temple, boldly claiming that he had fulfilled its words (Luke 4:14-21). Jesus understood that he came to offer God's forgiveness and hope to those held captive to sin and to bring God's justice to the poor and oppressed. That's the good news!

APPLY: How would you describe the mission statement for your life? If you can, take a few minutes to write it down.

PRAY: God, I want my life to count for you. Please help me to see clearly the mission you've called me to, and fill me with your Spirit to accomplish it.

DISCUSSION QUESTIONS FOR "MORE PROPHECIES ABOUT A SAVIOR"

1. For you, which of the prophecies in this section is the most significant proof that Jesus was the Messiah? Why?

2. The people of Israel felt the pressure of hostile armies on all sides; Jesus felt the pressure of being opposed and crucified. What pressures do you face for your beliefs, and how do you cope?

3. Have you ever felt that God has abandoned you? When? Do you ever feel that God is with you? When?

4. What tempts you to give up hope for the future? What things give you the most hope for the future?

5. Jesus said he came to bring good news to the poor, the prisoners, the blind and the oppressed? How could you be more like Jesus in this regard?

6. Why do you suppose it was necessary for Jesus to go through such incredible suffering?

7. Jesus seemed to claim the passage in Isaiah 61 as his personal mission statement. What's yours? (You may want to share your notes from reading 30.)

PART THREE

New Testament

The Birth of Jesus

SINCE 1965 WHEN IT FIRST APPEARED as a television special, *A Charlie Brown Christmas* may have done more to communicate the essence of the gospel than any thirty-minute sermon ever has. In the program Charlie Brown, the cartoon character from the *Peanuts* comic strip, searches for the true meaning of Christmas only to be disappointed and disillusioned. Finally, Charlie's thumb-sucking friend Linus walks onto an empty stage and recites from the Gospel of Luke, "For unto you is born this day in the city of David a Saviour, which is Christ the Lord" (Luke 2:11 KJV). Linus finishes by simply saying, "And that's what Christmas is all about, Charlie Brown."

In spite of the growing commercialization and secularization of the holiday season, most people today are still hungry to know what Christmas is all about. And that's exactly what our next five readings on the birth of Jesus will help us understand. We'll cover the familiar story of Joseph and Mary trekking to Bethlehem, of an unlikely birth in a manger, of the shepherds, angels and heavenly hosts all welcoming this special child.

One thing you'll notice is that the birth of Jesus was definitely not a random act; we see God clearly at work orchestrating this wonderful event. Several times God sends angels to announce important messages or to guide certain people at critical moments. When you think about it, the fact that this child was to be born of a virgin and destined to become the promised Messiah was a mind-boggling concept to accept. That had never happened before. God had to take special measures to communicate these truths.

You'll also notice several references to Old Testament prophecies. As we discovered in the earlier readings of *The Essential Jesus*, God had given many future clues, previews of coming attractions, that he was planning to send a Savior to the world. The good news is that the time had finally come. No more previews; it was finally time for the main event. God entered the world in the person of his Son, Jesus.

Finally, it's fascinating to examine how all the different people in these next readings reacted to the birth of Jesus. Joseph and Mary, the shepherds and wise men, the religious leaders and King Herod—all grappled with what was happening. Centuries later, we are able to more fully appreciate the truth as expressed in one of the names used to describe Jesus: Immanuel, "God with us." But don't take my word for it. You need to discover the true meaning of Christmas on your own. And that's what this next section is all about, Charlie Brown.

31 ❧ FAVOR WITH GOD

PRAY: "My soul glorifies the Lord and my spirit rejoices in God my Savior, for he has been mindful of the humble state of his servant" (Luke 1:46-48).

READ: Luke 1:26-56

REFLECT: How would you feel if an angel appeared to you? I'd like to think I'd be cool and stand my ground; more than likely, I'd just run. The Bible indicates that Mary was "greatly troubled" (v. 29) and afraid (v. 30), but at least she stayed and listened. Perhaps she sensed that this was a messenger from God (v. 26).

Mary is one of the great heroes of the Bible, a fact the angel confirms in the most incredible way (v. 30). But that raises an important question: how can we find favor with God today? Let's take a closer look at how Mary responded to this surprise visitor to see if we can find some clues.

First, we notice that she is *confident in her relationship to God*. She's not proud, nor is she falsely modest. She sees herself simply as "the Lord's servant" (v. 38). As followers of Jesus today, we too are favored by God, not because of anything we've done but rather because of what he's done for us (Ephesians 2:8-10). Mary demonstrates that God's uses people who have a humble confidence in him.

Second, we notice her *willingness to live by faith* (vv. 38, 45). She reminds us of another Bible hero, Abraham, who left everything to follow God's call (Genesis 12:1-9), a fact that reverberates throughout the Bible (Romans 4:3; Hebrews 11:8-12). Mary teaches us the power of believing and acting on God's Word.

Finally, we notice her *heart for God* (vv. 46-55). Mary's song (often called the Magnificat) is filled with Old Testament imagery and indicates that she was a young woman who had spent time reflecting on the Scriptures. Mary teaches us the value of being saturated in God's Word.

Our passage also contains one of the most popular verses in the Bible, "For nothing is impossible with God" (v. 37). Short and positive, it's sure to give us hope when life gets stressful. But seen in its context, the verse actually shows us that God intervenes in the lives of people, like Mary, who have developed a lifestyle of faithfully seeking him whether they are in the spotlight or not.

APPLY: Which of Mary's qualities do you see most in your life? Which do you want more of in your life?

PRAY: God, I want to seek more of you in my life, but I don't always know how to do that. Show me some practical ways I can find favor with you today.

32 ❧ JUST THE FACTS

PRAY: Lord God, as I read this passage in the Bible, I ask that you would communicate something new about Jesus to me.

READ: Matthew 1:18-25

REFLECT: You can tell this version of the birth of Jesus was written by an accountant (Matthew 10:3). Matthew began his Gospel with a genealogy (Matthew 1:1-17), not exactly a page-turner. Now he describes the most exciting event in the history of the world as if it's a footnote in a financial report, "before they came together, she was found to be with child" (Matthew 1:18). Helloooo. Is that all you can say?

But we shouldn't dismiss Matthew's perspective for its lack of dramatic flair. That's because he understood the most important thing: Jesus was born to save people from their sins (v. 21). There's no need to pump up a fact like that.

Another fact people struggle with today is the idea of the virgin birth (vv. 20-23). After all, we know science. We know biology. We know that could never happen, right? But just because something is beyond our understanding doesn't mean it couldn't be true. Notice that Matthew doesn't present the virgin birth as some easy-to-swallow fairy tale. Even Mary and Joseph had trouble grasping what was happening (Matthew 1:19; Luke 1:34). But that realistic struggle with the facts leads to a stronger faith and gives the Bible what scholar J. B. Phillips called "the ring of truth."

Perhaps the biggest fact that emerges from Matthew's report is that the birth of Jesus was no accident. It was all God's doing. As we see in this passage and several others related to Jesus' birth, God sent angels to explain his intentions and to direct the action when necessary. Not only that, as we discovered in our readings through the prophetic books and see again here, he had spoken through the prophets long before, predicting that these events would occur (Matthew 1:22-23).

Matthew's straightforward account of Jesus' birth leads us to one important conclusion: God is active in his world and he communicates to his people. And that's a fact.

APPLY: For you, what are the most important facts about Jesus? Are there any with which you still struggle?

PRAY: Spend a few minutes thanking God for the things you know about Jesus. Then ask him to help you understand the things about Jesus that aren't so clear to you now.

33 ∿ BLOCKBUSTER TRUTH

PRAY: Lord, the world seems out of control sometimes. But I'm so thankful to have the solid truth of your Word to give me perspective.

READ: Luke 2:1-40

REFLECT: If Matthew wrote like an accountant, Luke wrote like a screenwriter. His account of Jesus' birth captures the dramatic texture that makes for a good movie: the unique dilemma of the star couple (vv. 4-7), the comic relief of the confused shepherds (vv. 8-12, 16-20) and the grand spectacle of an angel choir (vv. 13-14). The Bible shows us that God used different personalities and perspectives to communicate many angles of the gospel truth.

I'm convinced that the most overlooked characters in this passage are the shepherds, and yet they seemed to come to the deepest understanding of what was really happening. Smelly and low on the economic totem pole of their day, shepherds weren't the kind of people you'd expect God to speak to. But God doesn't work just among the rich and famous. In fact, the Bible teaches that he has a special concern for the poor and oppressed (Psalm 35:10; 82:3-4; Proverbs 14:31), and so should we.

But it's how this unlikely supporting cast responded to the good news that is so instructive to us today. Note that the shepherds weren't too busy to investigate the claims about Jesus (Luke 2:15); they instinctively realized that finding Jesus was important, so they made it a priority (v. 16). Next, they didn't consider the truth about Jesus a private matter. Instead, they immediately began telling others what they had discovered (v. 17) and were unashamed to enthusiastically worship God (v. 20). Those are the marks of Jesus' true followers.

Luke 2:1-40 ends with cameo appearances by Simeon and Anna (vv. 25-38). In a modern movie these scenes might have ended up on the cutting room floor. But Luke included them because they are an important part of the story. God knew the events surrounding the birth of Jesus would seem unbelievable to Joseph, Mary and maybe even to us. So he confirms what he was doing through these prophecies. It reminds us that God has done everything he can think of to let us know the truth about his Son.

APPLY: Which character in the story of Jesus birth do you identify with the most? Why?

PRAY: Thank you, God, for going to such great lengths to communicate the truth about Jesus to me. Give me the courage to tell others the good news.

34 ❧ SEARCHING FOR JESUS

PRAY: God, I pray that as I read today you would help me understand the truth about who your Son Jesus really is.

READ: Matthew 2:1-23

REFLECT: In 1985 a group of liberal scholars founded the Jesus Seminar, supposedly to search for the real Jesus. Over the next decade, they isolated 176 events in the life of Jesus as reported in the Gospels, and then they voted on whether they thought each one really happened. The result? The scholars concluded that only 16 percent of the events did (or probably did) happen. But the Jesus Seminar scholars have been criticized over the years for their bias: it's hard to find the Son of God if you don't believe he exists.

In Matthew 2:1-23, the Magi, or wise men, embarked on an honest search for Jesus. They asked good questions, followed the evidence and remained open to the possibility that Jesus was the Messiah (v. 2). In the end they found and worshiped him (vv. 11-12). Herod, on the other hand, was already biased against Jesus (vv. 3, 16, 20), and his search for him was unsuccessful.

Another feature of this passage is the odyssey of Joseph and Mary. Think about it. They knew God was at work on their behalf; they had been visited by angels, shepherds and wise men. And they knew better than anyone else about the miraculous circumstances of Jesus' birth. Their boy was the promised Messiah. So it would be natural for them to think that life would be safe and secure. Not so. God's plan was to make them vulnerable refugees (vv. 13-15).

Sometimes being in the center of God's will means our lives won't be successful or easy; sometimes he needs us to travel the hard road. But we can be sure that no matter where he leads, God has a purpose in mind (Romans 8:28). In this case he was protecting this special family (vv. 19-20) and in the process fulfilling the plan he had announced centuries earlier (v. 23). God always knows what he is doing in our lives, even when his plan isn't so clear to us.

APPLY: What are some of the ways you've seen God work in your life over the years? Has he ever taught you something important from traveling the hard road?

PRAY: Think of the most difficult situation you face today. Spend some time asking God to show you what he is doing and to help you trust that he'll take care of you.

35 ❧ His Father's Son

PRAY: Heavenly Father, my mind is racing with everything I have to do. I need to slow down, slow down, slow down, so I can hear what you have to say to me today.

READ: Luke 2:41-52

REFLECT: I know exactly how Joseph and Mary felt (v. 48). I remember the time I lost track of our youngest daughter, Stephanie, in a large clothing store. She was about five years old, and after ten minutes of desperate searching I was going berserk. When I finally found her hiding and grinning in the middle of a circular rack of cloths, I felt a mixture of anger and relief.

But as we see in this passage, Jesus wasn't playing hide and seek in the temple. He was beginning to demonstrate the unique nature of who he was. Even as a preteen he possessed amazing wisdom far beyond his years (v. 47). It's as if this passage shows us what the greatest teacher the world has ever seen was like in Sunday school.

And notice how Jesus reacts to Mary's reference to "your father" (vv. 47-48). (I heard those words a few times growing up, although in a much different context, "When *your father* gets home . . .") Without missing a beat, Jesus responds, "Didn't you know that I had to be in my Father's house?" Jesus already understood that he was the divine Son of God. It wasn't a claim he invented later on to attract a crowd. He was born that way.

The interchange between Mary and Jesus also introduces us to a tension that builds throughout the Gospel accounts. Jesus often said things that assumed his divine nature and unique relationship to God. Some people missed his point or were confused by what he said. Other people clearly understood what Jesus meant and became angry or rejected him for it. That's how the religious leaders reacted to Jesus throughout his life. In fact, his words made them so angry over time that they finally killed him for it. I wonder if some of the leaders who chatted with Jesus in the temple that day were present twenty-one years later when he was crucified.

APPLY: What are your favorite statements of Jesus? Are there things Jesus said that you find hard to accept?

PRAY: Lord Jesus, whether your words are encouraging or challenging, I ask for the ability to honestly hear what you are saying to me.

DISCUSSION QUESTIONS FOR "THE BIRTH OF JESUS"

1. Throughout the account of Jesus' birth, God sends angels to announce good news and to direct the action. Why do you suppose he chose to do this?

2. Does God guide people today? If so, how? Can you give some examples?

3. When Jesus was born, the angel announced that it was good news. What exactly is the "good news"? Can you describe it in your own words?

4. Do you think most people know the real meaning of Christmas? How would you explain what Christmas is to a nonbelieving friend or co-worker?

5. Do you think people should lobby to have Jesus become more visible in Christmas decorations? What are some effective ways to put Christ into Christmas?

6. Have you ever had an experience that made no sense at the time but later convinced you that God was at work? What happened?

7. Why do you think Jesus' claim to be the Son of God would make some people angry?

The Beginning Ministry of Jesus

I ONCE WATCHED A TELEVISION DOCUMENTARY about the life of popular singer Bob Dylan. It was fun to see footage of the scruffy-haired star singing his greatest hits, including "Blowin' in the Wind," "The Times They Are A-Changin'," "Like a Rolling Stone" and many more. But the part of the program that most interested me was his early career, especially the year when he made the transition from an unknown folk singer named Robert Zimmerman in Minnesota to a "discovered" rock star in New York City named Bob Dylan.

Of course Jesus was far more than a rock star, but in our next five readings we'll be examining a similar transition period in his life as he goes from being an unknown carpenter from Nazareth to a popular preacher and healer who attracted big crowds. Unfortunately there is no television footage from those exciting days. But there is plenty of vivid detail captured in the Gospel accounts.

First, we'll look at what amounts to Jesus' public debut, his baptism. John the Baptist was creating quite a stir by preaching a tough message of repentance, and people were lining up to be dunked by him in the Jordan River. But when Jesus' turn came, God spoke loud and clear, "This is my Son, whom I love; with him I am well pleased" (Matthew 3:17). From the very beginning it was clear that Jesus was more than a carpenter.

That's why the devil attacked him right away in the desert, as we'll see next. We sometimes think temptation comes when we do the wrong thing or allow ourselves to get into the wrong situation. That's true enough. But temptation can also come when we are trying to do the right thing; Jesus was in the middle of a forty-day spiritual retreat. Either way, we'll learn how Jesus dealt with temptation, which is something that is incredibly helpful to know today.

Finally, as his ministry begins to pick up steam, we'll hear Jesus articulate his mission statement, we'll examine the nature of his ministry, and we'll watch as he begins recruiting his team. It's all exciting stuff.

One key theme that emerges from these early days of Jesus' ministry is his commitment to finding followers. In fact, throughout the Gospel accounts we see Jesus giving the simple challenge "Follow me." That little phrase was packed with a huge meaning, both for his original hearers and for us, as you are about to find out.

36 ∿ THIS IS MY SON

PRAY: "Praise be to the Lord, to God our Savior, who daily bears our burdens" (Psalm 68:19). Spend some time setting your burdens before the Lord.

READ: Matthew 3:1-17

REFLECT: I wonder if John the Baptist was a fun person to be around. Think about it: he was a negative conversationalist (v. 2) and had a knack for offending people (v. 7). Not only that, he was a weird dresser and had strange ideas about food (v. 4). He probably had bad breath too. How could such an odd duck become such a popular preacher (v. 5)? The answer is simple: he had a unique twofold message that people were hungry to hear.

Repent! The first part of his message had to do with repentance. John told people they were sinners, and he told them what to do about it (v. 8). You wouldn't think that would be such a popular theme. But to people weighed down by sin, a call to repentance is a blessing. If you've ever been forgiven for something you've done wrong you know what I'm talking about. Unconfessed sin has a way of eating us up from the inside out. But when we repent and finally get free of our guilt, we experience a sense of relief and joy. Perhaps those who think repentance is negative haven't tried it yet.

The kingdom of God is near! The second part of John's message had to do with Jesus; that's what he meant by saying "the kingdom of God is near." John the Baptist was the first person to publicly announce the fact that his younger cousin was actually the Messiah (John 1:29-34). That took a lot of humility (Matthew 3:11), but that was John's calling (v. 3).

All of this set the stage for a milestone event in the Gospel narrative (vv. 13-17). Although John didn't understand (v. 14), Jesus knew it was important for him to be baptized (v. 15) because it would become a unique demonstration of his divine nature (v. 17). And how interesting that all three persons of the Trinity were involved: the Son was baptized, the Holy Spirit descended and the Father spoke. Amen.

APPLY: Which part of John the Baptist's message applies the most to you now? To repent? Or that Jesus is near? Why?

PRAY: Lord Jesus, there are lots of things I don't understand, but I do want to get closer to you. Please show me the things that stand in the way of that.

37 ❧ DELIVER US FROM EVIL

PRAY: Heavenly Father, this world can be a dark and evil place at times. Please show me how I can be an instrument of your light.

READ: Luke 4:1-13

REFLECT: Do you believe in the devil? I do. I've never had an encounter with him, nor do I want to; but I have felt the presence of evil at times. I've also seen the effect of the devil's work in the lives of broken and destroyed people, and as we see in Luke 4:1-13, the devil was attempting to destroy Jesus in three ways.

The promise of granting physical desires. There's nothing wrong with food or eating in moderation. But the devil was trying to use Jesus' hunger to make him forget who he really was; note the taunt, "If you are the Son of God . . ." (v. 3). One of the devil's most effective strategies is to destroy people by causing them to take a natural desire to an evil extreme.

The promise of worldly power. This is the classic "deal with the devil" that has become the premise for so many plays and novels, "If you worship me, it will all be yours" (v. 7). Again, the drive to succeed is not wrong, taking it to extreme is. Those who are successful need people who can and will hold them accountable. Note that power and fame are tools the devil claims as his own (v. 6).

The promise of spiritual power. The devil returns to his original taunt (vv. 3, 9) but attaches it to a quote from Psalm 91. Perhaps spiritual temptations are the most subtle and dangerous. The devil doesn't need to stop us from doing God's work so long as he can get us to be ungodly as we do it. That still advances his evil agenda.

Jesus' didn't fall for any of these tactics. In each case he used his knowledge of the Scriptures to repel the devil's attack. And if Jesus needed God's Word to resist evil, we need it even more. Our struggle with temptation won't end (v. 13) until God deals with the devil once and for all (Revelation 20:10).

APPLY: To which of the three temptations Jesus faced do you feel most vulnerable? What's your strategy for resisting?

PRAY: Use the Lord's Prayer (Matthew 6:9-13) as your outline for prayer. Slowly say each phrase and add your own prayers to each.

38 ∿ Who's He Think He Is?

PRAY: "The grass withers and the flowers fall, but the word of our God stands forever" (Isaiah 40:8). Lord, open my eyes to something new from your eternal Word today.

READ: Luke 4:14-30

REFLECT: It must have been difficult to grow up around Jesus. The "soccer moms" no doubt had talked for years about the details of Mary's pregnancy and her son's birth. As Jesus grew up the religious teachers would have debated what this child prodigy was destined to become. And his friends from the neighborhood must have been flabbergasted when Jesus stepped into the spotlight at synagogue that day. Everyone who knew Jesus would have been wondering the same thing: *Who's he think he is?* The answer to that basic question begins to emerge in Luke 4:14-30. When Jesus stood up and read from the book of Isaiah, he was indicating at least two very important things about himself. The first was that he had a specific mission: "to preach good news to the poor" (v. 18). The Gospels help us understand that a person can be physically and spiritually poor (compare Matthew 5:3 with Luke 6:20). But either way, Jesus had come for them.

The second thing Jesus was saying is that he was more than a carpenter's son (v. 22). You'll remember from one of our earlier readings that the passage from Isaiah that Jesus read was one of four places in that book which describe the coming Messiah (the "Servant Songs"). By saying this Scripture had been fulfilled (v. 21), Jesus was clearly claiming he was that promised Messiah. You can imagine the stunned silence that followed. "Ah, right. Are there any other announcements today?"

Ever since, people have been divided about Jesus. Some accept him (v. 22) while others are infuriated by him (v. 28). And as you'll see in the rest of our journey through the Bible, Jesus made many more jaw-dropping statements about what he came to do (for example, John 5:24-27). A person who said what Jesus said and did what Jesus did demands a response.

APPLY: If you had been in the synagogue with Jesus that day, how do you think you would have reacted to his claim? Why?

PRAY: In your own words, complete this prayer, "Jesus, this is who I honestly think you are . . ."

39 ∽ WITH AUTHORITY!

PRAY: In spite of the stresses and problems that are in my life right now, Lord, I'm eager to read your Word because I know you have something to say to me.

READ: Luke 4:31-44

REFLECT: As a result of my work with Prison Fellowship, I became friends with a man named Aaron Johnson, a Baptist minister who had been appointed as the Secretary of Correction in North Carolina. After taking the job, his first decision was to ban swearing and pornography in all state prisons. When his lieutenants questioned the practicality of what he proposed, Rev. Johnson responded with a preacher's conviction, "Do I have the *authority* to make this decision?" "Well, yes you do, Mr. Secretary." "Fine! No more swearing or pornography in the prisons."

Our passage today shows Jesus going public with his ministry. No longer is he just a local "phenom"; he's starting to travel and attract crowds (vv. 31, 40-42). And as he does, the distinctive feature that is evident to all is his *authority*. We see it both in his preaching (v. 32) and in his healing (v. 36). We've already learned that Jesus was saturated in Scripture and empowered by the Spirit. No wonder he had such a powerful ministry.

It's significant that the demon-possessed heckler met Jesus in the synagogue, not in the back alley (v. 33). Today, we sometimes assume that churches are for "the good people." But if the church is doing its job, those who are disturbed or who have serious problems will also be attracted to the fellowship. Instead of rejecting or avoiding them, we need to introduce them to Jesus; he's the one with the authority to change their lives (v. 35).

Our passage gives us one other clue about the source of Jesus' authority, "At daybreak Jesus went out to a solitary place" (v. 42). In the hustle and bustle of his growing popularity, Jesus made time to be alone with God in prayer. Even though he was the Son of God, he made it a priority to talk with his Father. And that's a source of strength that's still available to us today.

APPLY: Imagine what it would have been like to be in the crowd listening to Jesus. How would you have felt? What would you have done?

PRAY: Spend some time alone with God, asking him for his power and strength as you face the challenges in your world.

40 ∿ THE LEADERSHIP STYLE OF JESUS

PRAY: Heavenly Father, I ask that you give me a clearer picture of who you are as I read your Word today.

READ: Luke 5:1-11

REFLECT: In the book titled *Managing for the Future*, business expert and author Peter Drucker makes this deceptively profound statement: "A leader is someone who has followers." His point is simply this: regardless of your title, what you wear or how you talk, regardless of any other management theory, if you can't motivate people to follow you, you're not a leader. In Luke 5:1-11, we get a unique insight into how the world's greatest leader recruited followers.

The first thing we notice is that the crowds were attracted to Jesus, not because he was a showman but rather because he was sharing "the word of God" (v. 1). That's still the key to church growth. As we read through the Gospels, we never get the sense that Jesus listened to his "handlers." In fact, he often baffled them by doing the opposite of what they thought would gain popularity (John 6:60, 66). But Jesus' goal was not popularity; it was to attract followers (Matthew 9:9; Mark 1:17; Luke 18:22; John 21:19).

The next thing we notice is how Jesus recruited followers one at a time, which is what Peter's experience shows us (Luke 5:4-11). Jesus took the trouble to communicate in a language Peter could understand: the fishing business. We make a mistake to think that God only works in a church or some other religious setting. God is at work everywhere in his world. Life takes on new meaning when we look for him in the details of our day.

The bulging nets convinced Peter he was in the presence of a higher power (v. 8). It's interesting that his first thought wasn't to snap a picture for the wall of his den: Peter and Jesus, arm in arm in front of the unbelievable mound of fish. Instead, he thought of his sin. That's what a real encounter with God does. It reveals the distance between God's holiness and our corruption. Even so, we have nothing to fear (v. 10). Jesus came to restore the relationship between sinful humans and a holy God. That's the reason to follow him.

APPLY: Do you ever feel afraid of God? Why?

PRAY: Lord, I ask that you would open my eyes to the ways that you are at work in the details of my day and life.

DISCUSSION QUESTIONS FOR "THE BEGINNING MINISTRY OF JESUS"

1. Do you think that God is pleased with you (Matthew 3:17)? Why?

2. Jesus spent forty days in the wilderness. Have you ever done something to help you get alone with God? What happened?

3. Jesus was tempted by the devil. Do you think the devil is active today?

4. Do you think the combination of fasting and praying is a healthy spir-

itual exercise? Why? What has been your experience with these disciplines?

5. Does the church you attend attract people who are disturbed or troubled? How could your congregation be more effective at introducing these and all people to Jesus?

6. What do you think it means to follow Jesus today?

7. Jesus challenged his followers to "Come, follow me . . . and I will send you out to fish for people" (Matthew 4:19 TNIV). What do you think he meant? How can we "fish for people" today?

The Sermons of Jesus

HOW MANY SERMONS HAVE YOU LISTENED TO IN YOUR LIFETIME?
Probably too many to count. I'm sure I've heard thousands, but I don't
know if I'll ever apply even half what I've heard. There's one thing, however, that I know for sure. I'd trade all the sermons I've ever heard just to
listen to one from Jesus. In our next five readings we'll have the privilege
of reading three major sermons of Jesus that we find in the Gospel
accounts.

The Sermon on the Mount (Matthew 5—7) is undoubtedly the most
famous sermon ever preached. Jesus delivered it at the beginning of his
public ministry and used it to spell out his view of the world. What we
notice right away is that Jesus' and our worldviews are radically different.
He starts with what has become known as the Beatitudes, a series of statements that might seem like devotional inspirations, until you actually
think about what he's saying. Jesus wants his followers to be poor in
spirit, meek, hungry for righteousness, merciful, pure in heart, committed to peacemaking and willing to endure persecution for living that way.
Hmm.

He goes on to set some incredibly high standards for his followers: we
should love our enemies, help the needy, stop worrying about money and
make his kingdom our first priority. In fact, at one point he even says, "Be
perfect, therefore, as your heavenly Father is perfect" (Matthew 5:48).
Maybe I'll just listen to that tape later.

In his next sermon we'll discover a hard edge to Jesus' preaching, which may come as a surprise. In his "Seven Woes" sermon, Jesus lays into the hypocrisy of the Pharisees and teachers of the law. He relentlessly pounds them for not practicing what they preached. But even in the midst of this angry tongue-lashing, Jesus never stops loving his listeners. As he says at the end of the sermon, "How often I have longed to gather your children together, as a hen gathers her chicks under her wings, but you were not willing" (Matthew 23:37).

In the final sermon we'll cover in this section, Jesus boldly predicts the end of the religious establishment of his day and then bridges to a description of the end of the world. It's a spellbinding sermon.

So hold onto your seat. You're about to listen to the words of the world's greatest preacher.

41 ❧ THE "NEW" REALITY

PRAY: Lord God, I want to know more about you so that I can live in a way that pleases you more. Please help me with that today.

READ: Matthew 5:1-48

REFLECT: What we now call the Sermon on the Mount has become the most famous sermon of all time. Some think it's just a collection of "blessed little moral statements." But a careful look reveals that Jesus preached about a large and challenging topic: the kingdom of heaven (referred to elsewhere in the Gospels as the kingdom of God). What exactly is it?

In general, the kingdom of heaven refers to God's rule on the earth. That's what Jesus came to announce and establish. And this will involve two distinct realities. The first is *internal*. Those who belong to the kingdom of heaven have a heart that is committed to the values that are important to God; they are humble, meek, merciful, peace-loving, righteous, pure and so on (vv. 3-10). Jesus says people like that will be rewarded by

God (v. 12). They will also be persecuted (v. 11) because those who live out God's values will stand out in contrast to the darkness and corruption of the world (vv. 13-16).

The second reality is *external*. Throughout the Old Testament, God's people were instructed to obey God's laws or suffer the consequences. That led to a system of legalism; just do the right thing and you're good with God. But note how Jesus repeats the phrase, "You have heard that it was said . . ." (vv. 21, 27, 31, 33, 38, 43). He's holding up various Old Testament laws and linking them to the new motivation of the kingdom of heaven. In essence he's saying, "It's not good enough to simply do the right thing; you need to do it for the right reason."

A new inner reality and a new external reality, that's what it means to belong to this new kingdom. That's what God had in mind all along (vv. 17-20).

APPLY: What motivates you to do the right thing?

PRAY: Which of the things mentioned in verses 3-10 would you like to see more of in your life? Make that the focus of your prayers.

42 ∾ HUNGRY FOR GOD

PRAY: Heavenly Father, I want to draw closer to you today in spite of the worries and pressures on me right now. Please lift them so I can sense your presence.

READ: Matthew 6:1-34

REFLECT: I remember the first time I read *Celebration of Discipline*, Richard Foster's book about the classic spiritual disciplines. I was eating lunch by myself in a McDonald's restaurant in downtown Philadelphia and was so moved that tears came to my eyes. I didn't realize it at the time, but I was hungry for more than a Big Mac. I wanted a deeper relationship with God, and Foster was describing a way to find it that was new for me.

I should have read the Sermon on the Mount too that day, because that's exactly the topic Jesus addresses in this passage: spiritual disciplines. He starts by discussing three that you would expect him to cover. About *giving* (vv. 1-4) he says it shouldn't be done for PR value; rather, we should keep a low profile. About *prayer* (vv. 5-15) he says the focus should be spending time alone with God. And about *fasting* (vv. 16-18) he says we shouldn't act like holier-than-thou martyrs.

I grew up thinking that when Jesus said "babbling like pagans" (v. 7), he meant those in liturgical churches who read the same prayers every week. I've since learned that extemporaneous prayer can be equally if not more like babbling if it's done for the wrong reason. Regardless of the spiritual discipline, the key, according to Jesus, is to focus on "your Father," not what people may think. Notice how many times he uses that phrase in this chapter.

Jesus concludes this section with two unexpected topics: *money* (vv. 19-24) and *worry* (vv. 25-34). We don't usually think of these as spiritual issues, but they often keep us from drawing closer to God. For me, worry is a much bigger problem than money. I worry about my children, my work, my health and the future. Sometimes I worry to show that I care; it seems like a "responsible" thing to do. But over the years, I've found that worry is emotionally and spiritually exhausting. That's why it helps to return again and again to the greatest spiritual discipline of all: "seek first his kingdom and his righteousness" (v. 33). That puts everything else into its proper perspective.

APPLY: Could you prove that God is the master of your life and that money isn't? How?

PRAY: Spend some time talking to God about the power of money and worry in your life. Ask him to show you how to make his kingdom your first priority.

43 ✎ THE GREAT COMMUNICATOR

PRAY: Heavenly Father, you know better than anyone what I need to hear right now. Please help me be open to a special communication from you in this passage.

READ: Matthew 7:1-29

REFLECT: Jesus broke all the rules for effective communicators. The Sermon on the Mount was long (way more than the average attention span of fifteen minutes), delivered outside (without a sound system) and included no jokes (or even a funny story).

But Jesus amazed the crowds because he had the one thing no communication coach could ever teach: authority (v. 29). The Son of God was able to communicate the word of God like no one else could, and in this last portion of the Sermon on the Mount Jesus zeroes in on three main points.

Judging others: Don't do it! Christians must walk a fine line on this issue; on one hand they must hate sin, but on the other, they must love the sinner. Easier said than done. Perhaps that's why Jesus suggested that we focus on removing our own sins first; if we do, there won't be much time for anything else.

Seeking God: Do it! Some people seem to have an "entitlement mentality" when it comes to God; they think he owes them something whether they believe in him or not. But Jesus counsels a proactive approach to finding God (vv. 7-8): God blesses those who sincerely seek him (vv. 9-11; see also Hebrews 11:6).

False prophets: Watch out! Our world is full of religious gurus who seem good but in fact are dangerous (Matthew 7:15); following the wrong one can have serious consequences (vv. 22-23). To prevent this, we first need to evaluate the actions ("fruit" [v. 16]) of any teacher. Next we need to determine if their message is consistent with God's will, which for us is most clearly expressed in the Bible.

Jesus wraps up the world's greatest sermon with a straightforward analogy about houses built on sand and rock. The point? Build your life on the rock-solid words of Jesus. Nothing complicated about that.

APPLY: Do you feel that other people unfairly judge you? When and why? How could you become more accepting of others without condoning their sins?

PRAY: Spend a few moments confessing your sins to God. Are there any things that need to removed from your eyes?

44 ❧ No More Mr. Nice Guy

PRAY: Heavenly Father, I love having your Word as a reference point. Please guide me through what I read today.

READ: Matthew 23:1-39

REFLECT: Niccolo Machiavelli (1469-1527) was an Italian political thinker who gained lasting notoriety for, among other things, his "end justifies the means" philosophy and his dislike of Christianity. In Machiavelli's view, Jesus was too humble and weak to make an impact in the real world.

But perhaps Machiavelli should have read Matthew 23:1-39. In it, he would have encountered a passionate, angry Jesus who had no trouble getting in the face of his opponents when necessary. It's a misconception to think that being a Christian means you have to act like a wimp. Biblical characters are often encouraged to become "strong and courageous" (Joshua 1:7; 1 Chronicles 28:20). The key, however, is to be sure we are pursing God's agenda, not our own, when we do.

So what got Jesus so ticked off? The answer boils down to a single word: *hypocrisy.* The teachers of the law and Pharisees (the name for a group of religious leaders within Judaism at the time) weren't practicing what they preached (Matthew 23:3). Notice the strong language

Jesus used: "blind guides" (v. 16), "blind fools" (v. 17), "snakes" and "brood of vipers" (v. 33). No one likes a hypocrite.

In fact, the tension between Jesus and these leaders had been building for a long time (Luke 4:28-30; 6:11). In the previous chapter they tried to trap and discredit Jesus (Matthew 22:15, 18). Even though they seemed like holy men, their motives were clear to Jesus (Matthew 12:14). True holiness doesn't come from a fancy religious title or from acting like a saint. There are many things we can do to appear holy, but that's all it is, an appearance. True holiness requires a complete harmony between God's priorities and our actions (Matthew 23:23).

Machiavelli thought that strong people were those who ruthlessly did whatever necessary to maintain power and authority, even if it meant lying and deception. Jesus demonstrated that true strength involves standing up for God's agenda, no matter what the circumstances.

APPLY: Is there a situation in your life where you could stand up for God's agenda? How could you do so?

PRAY: Lord, help me to be strong and courageous for you in the challenges I face.

45 ✅ THE END

PRAY: Lord, I ask that you would help me see the world and my life from your perspective as I read your Word today.

READ: Matthew 24:1-51

REFLECT: Jesus got into big trouble for his little sound bite about the temple (vv. 1-2); it seemed like he was planning a terrorist attack on the most revered structure in all of Judaism, and the religious leaders never forgave him for it (Matthew 26:61). Although there's no direct comparison today, it would be something like a person publicly claiming his intention to blow up the National Cathedral, the U.S. Capitol and the White House all at once. People would get pretty touchy.

But Jesus wasn't really talking about a physical building; he was talking about his "body," the church, that is, all those who believe in and follow him (John 2:19-22). That's what would replace the stone temple, impressive though it was. The disciples had trouble grasping all of this (Matthew 24:3), so later Jesus took time to explain, which is what the bulk of Matthew 24 is all about. A careful examination of what Jesus said in this private sermon reveals that he had at least three perspectives in mind.

He was predicting that the temple would eventually be destroyed (v. 2), but he wouldn't be the one to do it. As it turned out, the Roman legions took care of that when they burned it to the ground in A.D. 70. For starters, Jesus was saying, "Don't put your faith in bricks and mortar or anything else in this world; it's all temporary."

He was predicting his disciples were in for some tough times (vv. 4-14); they would be "persecuted and put to death, and . . . hated" (v. 9). Soon after Jesus' death and resurrection, that's exactly what happened. His followers were persecuted, first by some Jews (Acts 8:1-3) and then by the Romans. Jesus was saying that following him won't always be a bed of roses. That's still true today.

He was predicting the end of the world (vv. 15-51). Again, it will be a time of great stress and worldwide tumult; some say it has begun to happen today. But the followers of Christ have nothing to fear because regardless of what happens or when it does, the most important thing is that Jesus will one day return. Jesus was saying that we should be ready and waiting for that day (v. 44).

APPLY: Are you ready and waiting for the return of Jesus? In what ways?

PRAY: Father in heaven, I ask that you help me focus more on what is eternal and less on what is temporary in my life.

DISCUSSION QUESTIONS FOR "THE SERMONS OF JESUS"

1. Do you think the Beatitudes (Matthew 5:1-12) are just ideals, or do you think we should really try to live that way today?

2. Should Christians ever have enemies? Why?

3. Share your experiences with practicing the spiritual disciplines mentioned in this section—fasting and prayer.

4. Jesus said, "Do not worry about your life" (Matthew 6:25). Talk about how you're doing with that challenge.

5. Which has a greater hold on your life—God or money? What's your evidence?

6. What examples of hypocrisy have you seen in the church? What examples of hypocrisy have you seen in your life?

7. How does the fact that the world will end and Jesus will someday return affect your life and decisions?

The Parables of Jesus

I USED TO GIVE CHILDREN'S SERMONS AT OUR CHURCH in Philadelphia. In the middle of the service, all the kids in the congregation were invited to the front rows. My job was to deliver a three to five minute talk that captured the essence of what our pastor would later preach to the grownups.

The first few times didn't go too well. The kids wiggled and giggled and didn't listen to anything I had to say. That's because I was boring; I simply told them what they were supposed to do. "Be good. Always obey your parents. Blah, blah, blah."

Then one Sunday I told the children a story about a time when I had done something wrong as a child and what I learned from it. They loved it and gave me their full attention. So the next time I did the children's sermon, I told another story with similar results. Pretty soon that's all I did, tell stories about "naughty little Whitney."

After a while I noticed something else: the adults liked my stories too. They'd come up to me during the coffee hour to talk about what I said and to tell me their stories. One time, a church elder told me, "You know, Whitney, you've become quite the raconteur." I had no idea what a raconteur was; all I knew was he liked my stories.

As you'll see in our next five readings, Jesus used stories or parables all the time in his ministry. In fact, judging from the material recorded in the four Gospels, he spent more time telling stories than he did preaching. Sometimes this teaching style perplexed his disciples; they once asked him flat out, "Why do you speak to the people in parables?" (Matthew 13:10). He did it first of all because stories communicate, and second because he was speaking to such a wide variety of people. Some of his listeners were devoted followers, some were arch enemies, some were confused onlookers, some were hurting souls and some, like you and me, would only read his words centuries later. But all of us could relate to a good story.

So get ready. You are about to explore the parables of Jesus, the world's greatest storyteller.

46 ∾ HAVE MERCY!

PRAY: Father God, my heart's desire is to understand and experience you more today. Please help me do that as I think about your Word today.

READ: Luke 10:25-37

REFLECT: Recently I attended a discussion with an expert on global climate change. Although I'm convinced this is a very serious issue, I left early because many in the audience weren't interested in hearing what the scientist had to say. Instead, they wanted to draw attention to themselves by asking smart-sounding questions.

That's the challenge Jesus faced in this impromptu Q & A session. Initially, the expert in the law wasn't interested in spiritual things; his intent was "to test Jesus" (v. 25). Even so, Jesus allowed him his fifteen seconds of fame; I imagine the tone of verse 26 to be something like this: "Okay, Mr. Know-It-All, why don't you show everyone how well you know the Scriptures." But Jesus knew that beneath the man's desire to show off was a deeper need; he wasn't sure of his relationship with God (v. 29).

Perhaps the expert was retreating to safer theological ground with his follow-up question about neighbors (v. 29). But Jesus' goal was not to debate theology; it was to show us what God is like. In this situation he does so by telling the wonderful story we call the parable of the good Samaritan

(vv. 30-35). In it, the Levite and the priest, the religious experts of that time, failed to do what the Scriptures taught or what God wanted. On the other hand, the Samaritan, the mixed-race outcast of that time, obeyed the Scriptures and pleased God. The point is that if you want to know God you need to have mercy.

Why? Because having mercy is the reason God sent his Son to earth. Like the good Samaritan, Jesus went out of his way to find us. Like the good Samaritan Jesus paid the price to restore us. And like the good Samaritan Jesus made an enormous sacrifice to save us. In spite of his impressive theological knowledge, the expert in the law didn't have a clue about God's mercy. The only way to do that is to understand what happened on the cross.

APPLY: Are there situations in your life where you could have mercy? What would that look like?

PRAY: Heavenly Father, having mercy sounds good in general but it's difficult to live out. Please help me show mercy is one specific situation this week.

47 ❧ RICH TOWARD GOD

PRAY: Heavenly Father, more than anything else, I desire to have a deeper relationship with you. Please show me how I can do that today.

READ: Luke 12:13-21

REFLECT: Talk about chutzpah! This man had the guts to interrupt Jesus in front of "many thousands" (Luke 12:1) with a complaint about his estate plan (v. 13). You can almost hear the frustration in Jesus' voice (v. 14). But before we come down too hard on this poor brother, we need to ask if our money and possessions have ever caused us to lose sight of the more important things in life. No comment.

So what did Jesus say to this man (and other distracted followers like us) about money and possession?

Jesus puts his finger on the root problem: Greed (v. 15). Years later, the apostle Paul said the same thing: "For the love of money is a root of all kinds of evil" (1 Timothy 6:10). It's true that we need resources in order to survive. But Jesus warned that they can easily pull our hearts over the edge into greed, so we need to watch out.

Jesus reminds us that life is more than possessions (v. 15). I'll say "amen" to that every time, but honestly I find it's easier said than done. On Saturday mornings I love to drink a cup of coffee while looking at the glossy advertising inserts in the weekend paper. The funny thing is, when I'm done I often get this overwhelming urge to go buy something, anything. I know life is more than possessions, but . . .

Jesus illustrates his point with a story about a rich fool (vv. 16-20), which could be summarized like this: he who dies with the most toys . . . still dies. And notice that it wasn't the man who produced the incredible wealth for himself. Rather, "the ground" produced it (v. 16). Jesus' point is very clear: Even our ability to produce wealth is a gift from God. It all belongs to him. Our goal in life should not be to amass great wealth for ourselves. Rather, we should focus on becoming "rich toward God" (v. 21) and that will require us "to do good, to be rich in good deeds, and to be generous and willing to share" (1 Timothy 6:18).

APPLY: What are some practical ways you can live a life that is "rich toward God"?

PRAY: God, I thank you for the many material blessings you've given to me. Please show me how I can use them in a way that pleases you.

48 ✌ HAPPY MEAL

PRAY: Lord, please give me a deeper awareness of your presence as I read, reflect and pray.

READ: Luke 14:1-24

REFLECT: It's difficult to understand Jesus' parable about a great banquet (vv. 16-24) without first appreciating the tense situation he was in when he told it (vv. 1-15): a dinner party with an influential group of his enemies. Let's not miss the fact that Jesus engaged with those who didn't agree with him; he ate with them and prayed for them (Matthew 5:44).

But he also got angry with them for caring more about their petty rules (v. 3) than for a needy person (v. 2). When do's and don'ts become more important to us than showing compassion, we've lost touch with God's priorities, no matter how correct our rules may be. Religion based only on "being right" looks good on the outside, but it leads to pride on the inside (v. 7).

In the midst of the tension, someone blurts out a holy-sounding statement about a feast in the kingdom of God (v. 15), perhaps thinking this "happy meal" was a wonderful example of what it will be like. Jesus responds with a parable that makes one thing clear: the kingdom of God will be nothing like this tense, exclusive dinner party.

So what does Jesus teach about the kingdom of God from this parable? First, God's intent is for all people to get in; the banquet host goes to extraordinary lengths to make it possible for everyone to attend (vv. 17, 21, 23). Second, God's kingdom is not just for the wealthy and talented or for those who have their act together; the banquet host also makes a special effort to include the down-and-outers, "the poor, the crippled, the blind and the lame" (v. 21). Finally, it is possible to reject God's invitation (vv. 18-20, 24). These fictional excuses may sound silly, but they communicate an important truth: there's never a good reason for rejecting God's invitation.

Some day, God will host a great fellowship banquet for all those who have chosen to follow Jesus. What a happy meal that will be!

APPLY: How could you take the initiative to engage with people that don't agree with you?

PRAY: Think of one person with whom you disagree. Spend some time praying for that person.

49 ～ SINNERS WELCOME!

PRAY: Lord, please show me anything that stands in the way of drawing closer to you.

READ: Luke 15:1-32

REFLECT: My church is located on a very busy road. Because of that, we sometimes put up a huge sign over the main entrance that says "Welcome!" We want to attract as many people as we can to worship with us. But after reading today's passage I wonder if we should change the sign to say, "Sinners Welcome!" I'm not sure if that would attract more or less people.

I am sure that Jesus would love the change because sinners were the focus of his ministry, a point that confounded the religious leaders (v. 2). They thought religion should be reserved only for "good people" like themselves. But Jesus demonstrated that true religion was for bad people; all of us are sinners (Romans 3:23). That's a tough nut for anyone to swallow, so Jesus told three parables to explain what he meant.

The first two, about a *lost coin* and a *lost sheep* (vv. 3-10), are fairly straightforward. If you've ever misplaced a large amount of cash or lost a beloved pet, you can understand the feelings Jesus is describing. That's how God feels about sinners. He knows they're lost and he really wants to find them. That's good news.

The third parable, about the *prodigal (wasteful) son* (vv. 11-32), is more personal and adds a plot twist: sin. The younger brother willfully does all the wrong things and deserves to be punished. As he blubbers on with a rehearsed apology (vv. 18-19), the suspense builds as we wonder how the father will react. Will it be the cold shoulder, an angry tongue lashing or complete rejection? It's none of these. The father responds with joy over a sinner who has come home (vv. 22-24). In fact, the theme that unites the three parables is joy (vv. 6-7, 9, 23); God rejoices when sinners repent (vv. 7, 10). That's even more good news.

But here's the catch: to experience that joyful reunion with God, you've got to admit that without him you're lost. You've must come to grips with your own sin. That's something the older brother (and the religious leaders) were unwilling to do (vv. 25-30). But it's the necessary first step to a relationship with God.

APPLY: With which character can you identify more: the younger or the older brother? Why?

PRAY: Heavenly Father, please forgive me for the times when I act like the older brother. Thank you that you are willing to welcome me back with open arms.

50 ❧ UNCOMMON PRAYER

PRAY: Lord Jesus, you took time to teach your disciples to pray. I ask that you would help me get a better understanding of how to communicate with you.

READ: Luke 18:1-14

REFLECT: When I was in high school, I loved English class (well, most of the time) because we got to study short stories. I enjoyed seeing how great authors could develop memorable characters and interesting plots in just a few pages. That's exactly what Jesus does in the two parables we read today.

The first one, about the *persistent widow* (vv. 1-8), was directed toward the disciples and anyone else who wants to follow Jesus. There's a bit of humor in the interplay between the corrupt judge and the pesty woman. The surprising thing is that Jesus held this tireless agitator up as his model prayer warrior. But effective prayer doesn't always sound like it comes from the Book of Common Prayer. Often it involves insisting, pleading and begging with God. It's important to note, however, that the woman's cause is consistent with God's priorities; she's praying for justice

(v. 3), not a new Cadillac.

The second parable, about the *Pharisee and the tax collector* (vv. 9-14), was directed to anyone who is proud and condescending (v. 9). The obvious point is that God responds to the prayers of humility, not pride. The tricky thing is to know the difference, and that's not always so easy to do. Getting involved in church, avoiding sin, pursuing spiritual disciples are all good things—unless they cause us to look down on others. Prayers based on our own goodness don't get too far with God. Prayers based on our need for him get a much better reception.

Maybe these parables are less like a collection of short stories and more like another volume on my shelf at home. It's called *The Book of Uncommon Prayer*, and it contains a collection of unorthodox but honest prayers through the ages. Jesus seems to be saying that whatever they sound like, those are the ones God likes best.

APPLY: Do you feel that you are honest with God when you pray? Why?

PRAY: Take a few minutes to say or even write out your own uncommon prayer.

DISCUSSION QUESTIONS FOR "THE PARABLES OF JESUS"

1. What examples of showing mercy have you seen or experienced recently?

2. Some people think that showing mercy is a sign of weakness. What do you think?

3. What's your philosophy about money and possessions? Is it really possible to be wealthy but not "possessed by your possessions"?

4. How could you use the resources God has given you for maximum return according to his priorities?

5. What practical steps could you take to show more compassion for the "down-and-outers" in your world?

6. Was there ever a time in your life when you felt lost and away from God? What was it like? Have you made your way back to him yet? If so, how did it happen?

7. When is pride a good thing? How do you know when pride is bad and how can you avoid it?

More Parables of Jesus

AS WE DISCOVERED IN THE LAST FIVE READINGS, Jesus used parables all the time in his teaching ministry. He'd tell an interesting story and use it to communicate an important or sometimes threatening truth to his listeners.

In our next five readings, we'll cover another set of parables based on two topics. The first is perhaps the greatest theme that emerges from Jesus' parables: the kingdom of heaven. We've already established a basic definition of that mysterious phrase: God's rule on the earth (see chap. 41). But that's sounds too much like a quote from a theology book. We'll understand it much better when we read the stories Jesus told.

When you do, you'll notice that Jesus never said, "The kingdom of heaven is exactly this _____. Period!" Instead, he said, "The kingdom of heaven *is like . . .*" and then he connected it to a good short story. That's because there is so much to understand. Each of the ten parables about the kingdom of heaven (some are very short, so we'll read several at a time) gives us a different insight into this major theme. At the end, you'll need to piece everything together. It's like assembling a jigsaw puzzle; after a while you can begin to see the full picture.

The second topic in this section is actually a variation of the parable teaching method. John called it a "figure of speech" (John 10:6). Instead of telling a full-blown story with a plot and a punch line, Jesus pointed his listeners to a familiar object—a shepherd, a flock of sheep, a gate, a vine, some branches, a gardener—and used the analogy to explain deep truth.

Whether it's a story or figure of speech, there's a lot to learn from the parables of Jesus. So let's get back to it.

51 ❧ It's Like . . .

PRAY: Lord, you know the clutter that fills my heart and mind today. Please enable me to look beyond that to what you want me to see in your Word.

READ: Matthew 13:1-58

REFLECT: As we sort through the collection of six parables in Matthew 13, it will help to remember our basic definition of the kingdom of heaven, since that's the theme that holds this chapter together. In essence, the kingdom of heaven is God's rule on the earth, or his territory and his people (see chap. 41).

Perhaps the most famous of these parables is the first, about "the sower" (vv. 3-9). Jesus' description of a solitary farmer spreading seed by hand has been the subject of great paintings by Jean-François Millet (1851), Vincent van Gogh (1888) and many others. And even though most of us don't live in agrarian societies today, Jesus' reflections on where the seed fell still communicates an important truth about the Word of God: it must be received and nurtured in order to bear fruit in our lives.

Taken together, these parables help us see a more complete picture of the kingdom of heaven. It starts small (like seeds) and has a unique power to grow (like a mustard seed or yeast). It's worth everything you have to obtain (like hidden treasure or a pearl) and eventually will include many, many people (like a net). There's only one dark cloud on this beautiful canvas: some will oppose the kingdom of heaven and its inhabitants (like weeds). It's amazing how much truth Jesus packed into a few word sketches.

But all this raises an interesting question: Why did Jesus rely so much on parables (v. 10)? The answer has to do with our willingness to receive his message. To learn from Jesus' parables requires that we receive his message with humility and faith, which is something many of his listeners lacked (v. 58). By quoting from Isaiah (vv. 14-15) Jesus is saying that those who understand with their heads only, that is, without believing, don't really understand it at all. To enter the kingdom of heaven requires knowledge and belief. That's what it means to "understand with your heart" (v. 15).

APPLY: What word picture would you use to describe your understanding of the kingdom of heaven? It's like _____.

PRAY: Jesus, I do want to be included in your kingdom. Please increase my knowledge and strengthen my belief in who you are and what you offer me.

52 ∿ THE GENEROUS LANDOWNER

PRAY: Lord God, sometimes I wonder how I could make my relationship with you more real and vital. I ask you to show me ways to do that today.

READ: Matthew 20:1-16

REFLECT: The punch line of the parable of the generous landowner is familiar to most people (v. 16). You might hear it quoted as a joke when someone cuts into line at a church supper. "Well you know, the last will be first, and the first will be last." But the parable and its point were no joke to Jesus. Through them he was communicating another important point about the kingdom of heaven (v. 1). What did he have in mind?

The parable seems easy to understand at first: workers are hired at different points throughout the day with the promise of fair wages at the end. The suspense builds as the early birds anticipate how much overtime pay they might collect. But that's were the plot gets complicated; everyone receives the same amount. Those who worked twelve hours are paid the same as those who worked one. Now we are really confused. Is the landowner fair or unfair? Is he a rich oppressor or a heartless communist?

But Jesus is using this seeming unfairness to make his point. The kingdom of heaven cannot be earned; it's a gift from God (Ephesians 2:8-9). Instead of calling this "the parable of the workers in the vineyard," it might be more accurate to call it "the parable of the generous landowner" (v. 15). That's because Jesus was saying our salvation is dependent on God's generosity, not on our good works.

That was a tough message for the religious experts of Jesus' day to accept. After all, they led the chosen people. They scrupulously followed all God's commands and regulations. If anyone deserved to get into the kingdom of heaven, it was them. But religion based on human effort and earning salvation leads away from God and into pride.

The truth is, God wants everyone to enjoy the benefits of his kingdom. Instead of grumbling about who deserves to be in or out (vv. 11-12), the workers would have done better to celebrate with the generous landowner at the end of the day. That's what it will be like in the kingdom of heaven.

APPLY: Which image best describes your view of the Christian faith: a rule book or a Christmas gift? Why?

PRAY: Lord Jesus, I can never repay you for what you did on the cross, but I am very, very grateful.

53 ❧ I Wanna Be Ready

PRAY: Before you read Matthew 25:1-46, take a minute to prayerfully reflect on 1 John 4:15-18.

READ: Matthew 25:1-46

REFLECT: I like parables that make a spiritual point with an everyday example. And I especially like it when Jesus zings the religious leaders of his day. But Matthew 25 makes *me* squirm. Darkness, weeping, gnashing of teeth and eternal punishment (vv. 30, 46)—these parables are definitely not bedtime reading. What's gotten into Jesus?

Actually, he's just completing his picture of the kingdom of heaven (vv. 1, 14). In earlier parables Jesus made the point that God invites everyone to enter his kingdom. But now he says some won't accept that invitation; some will be left out and it won't be God's fault. Each of the ten virgins had an opportunity to get ready for the bridegroom; five used it wisely and five let it slip away (vv. 1-13). All three of the servants received an investment from the wealthy man; two made the most of it and one misused it (vv. 14-30).

The last parable is perhaps the most sobering of all (vv. 31-46). It envisions a final day of reckoning when the Son of Man will sort out the sheep from the goats, that is, he'll determine who will enter the kingdom of heaven and who will not. At first reading it might seem like Jesus is saying we *can* earn our salvation after all, if we just help the homeless, hungry, imprisoned and needy. But we can't see this parable in isolation from his earlier teaching. First, we must accept and believe in Jesus, that is, we must "understand with our hearts" (Matthew 13:15). Then we must demonstrate the reality of that belief through our compassionate actions. It's the same thing the apostle James said many years later (James 2:26).

Some people find the idea of a final judgment difficult to accept; they feel that hellfire-and-brimstone preaching is manipulative. Unfortunately it can be. But that doesn't eliminate the reality that Jesus will someday return to judge humankind. And no matter how we may feel about it, the best response is this: use your time now to get ready. Then you'll hear God say, "Well done, good and faithful servant."

APPLY: How do you feel about a final day of judgment? What are you doing to get ready?

PRAY: Lord, sometimes the idea of judgment makes me fearful. Please reassure me with a deeper sense of your love today.

54 ❧ ONE WAY

PRAY: Heavenly Father, I long to hear your voice. Please help me listen with my heart as I spend time with you and your Word.

READ: John 10:1-18

REFLECT: At different points in his teaching ministry, Jesus used a variation of the parable style of teaching to communicate with his listeners. He used a "figure of speech" (v. 6). Instead of telling a story, he presented word pictures or analogies and then used them to describe several nuances of a spiritual truth. In our reading today, we find two of these—a gate to a sheep pen and a good shepherd.

The gate. The point of the gate analogy is straightforward: Jesus is the entry point into God's kingdom (v. 9). I once taught a Sunday school class for middle school boys; they had trouble sitting still but asked lots of good questions about Jesus. Sometime later, two parents publicly criticized me for "imposing" on the class my belief that Jesus is the only was to salvation. My reaction was this: "I'm sorry, but that's not just my belief; it's what Jesus said."

The good Shepherd. The second analogy, about the good shepherd, is more familiar. As we've seen earlier in our journey, the Bible often uses the image of a shepherd and sheep to communicate God's relationship with his people (Isaiah 40:11; Ezekiel 34:12). In this passage Jesus emphasizes two details of the picture. The first is the shepherd's *voice*. Jesus' followers can enjoy close relationship with him (John 10:14); they will recognize his voice (vv. 4-5). He is not an impersonal "higher being." He knows your name (v. 3); he cares about you like a shepherd who recognizes and loves his sheep. The second detail is the shepherd's willingness to *sacrifice* himself (vv. 11, 15). Jesus is clearly foreshadowing what he would later do on the cross.

It's baffling that some felt threatened by Jesus' teaching and chose to reject him (v. 20). But that still happens today. How sad that people are more willing to accept a distant, impersonal God rather than accepting

Jesus' offer of new life: "I have come that they may have life, and have it to the full" (v. 10).

APPLY: Why do you think some people have so much trouble believing that Jesus is the only way to God?

PRAY: Spend some time praying for one person you know who's struggling with the idea that Jesus is the way to God.

55 ❧ THE VINEYARD CHURCH

PRAY: Heavenly Father, I am so thankful that you are in charge of this world and my life. I come into your presence today confident that you know what's best for me.

READ: John 15:1-17

REFLECT: It's important to understand the context in which Jesus introduced this next figure of speech. In John 14—17, John records an extended, private teaching session that Jesus had with his disciples the night before he was arrested (chap. 18) and then crucified (chap. 19). John 15:1-17 is part of Jesus' last opportunity to communicate the nature of his relationship with his Father and his followers. It was a tough challenge, so he used a familiar image—a vine and its branches.

Let's start by clarifying the basics; Jesus says he's the vine (v. 1), his followers are the branches (v. 5) and God is the gardener (v. 1). That would be easy to remember. But think about all the things that such a simple analogy would communicate: The gardener is in charge. The vine holds everything together. The branches can't live apart from the vine. What other lessons do you see?

Jesus goes on to emphasize two specific points about the analogy that he felt were especially important. The first was the significance of *fruit*. The main job of the branches was to bear fruit, that is, for Jesus' followers to do the things he's been instructing them to do (vv. 7-8). That's still true today. The most important thing we can do in life is not be successful or wealthy or recognized. It's to bear "fruit that will last" (v. 16). Is that the goal of your life?

His second point relates to *love*. Jesus didn't encourage his disciples with some Disney-style platitude: Just follow your hearts. Instead, he commanded them to love one another (v. 17). That's tough work, especially since he set the ultimate standard (v. 13). True love involves both obedience to God's commands and sacrifice for the good of others. Is that kind of love evident in your life?

The kitchen window in our house looks out over one of my wife's many gardens. On the window sill she keeps a little plaque with a quote on it based on Dorothy Frances Gurney's poem "God's Garden." The plaque reads: "One is closer to God in a garden than anywhere else on earth." I think Jesus just might agree.

APPLY: Which goal do you need to work on more in the next month: bearing fruit or showing love? How could you do this?

PRAY: Ask God for his help in working on the goal you've selected apply.

DISCUSSION QUESTIONS FOR "MORE PARABLES OF JESUS"

1. Have you ever seen or experienced examples of the kingdom of heaven here on earth? What was it like?

2. Why do you think most of the religions of the world are based on the idea that we can somehow earn salvation?

3. If salvation is really a gift from God, is there any need for good works? Why bother to be good if you can't earn your salvation?

4. Do you think preaching and teaching about judgment should have greater or lesser emphasis in churches today? Why?

5. Today, some people are offended by the idea that Jesus is the only way to God? What do you think? Is it acceptable to express this view in public?

6. In what ways should a Christian bear fruit? Should all believers bear the same kind of fruit? Is there some fruit that all followers of Christ should have?

7. What are the best examples of sacrificial love that you've seen in your lifetime?

The Miracles of Jesus

THOMAS JEFFERSON WAS FASCINATED BY JESUS. He believed that the ethical teachings of Jesus were the greatest the world had ever known. As a result, Jefferson created a book titled *The Life and Morals of Jesus of Nazareth*. In it, he sorted through every verse in the four Gospels and extracted only those which he thought expressed the pure principles of Jesus. He then arranged the selected verses into chronological order. Over time the volume became known as *The Jefferson Bible* and for many years it was distributed to every new member of the U.S. Congress.

But a review of *The Jefferson Bible* today quickly reveals that something very important is missing: Jefferson removed all references to Jesus' miracles or to his resurrection. Although Thomas Jefferson believed Jesus was a great moral teacher, he simply couldn't accept the supernatural aspects of his life and ministry.

In our next ten readings, we'll consider the miracles of Jesus. The first set is a collection of five "supernatural events"—changing water into wine, calming the seas, feeding more than five thousand people from a few loaves of bread and fish, walking on water, and causing a fig tree to wither. In fact, all of Jesus' miracles could be called supernatural, but this first set highlights his power to overrule the forces of nature. In the second set we'll cover six healing miracles of Jesus. Once we've completed these readings, which cover much of the material Thomas Jefferson removed from his "Bible," we'll see why the miracles are an indispensable part of the essential Jesus.

We'll also discover that Jesus performed miracles for a variety of reasons. Of course at the most basic level, Jesus wanted to meet the needs of the people around him: his disciples, the crowds and the individual followers along the way. But beyond that Jesus' miracles were signs that had two other purposes. As John tells us at the end of his account of Jesus' first miracle, turning water into wine (John 2:1-11), they revealed his glory and they helped people put their faith in him. Jesus' miracles were intended to help people believe that he was the Son of God, which is why it's important not to skip over them.

56 ❧ NEW WINE

PRAY: Heavenly Father, sometimes my understanding of you seems tired and stale. I pray that you'd guide me toward a fresh, new relationship with you today.

READ: John 2:1-11

REFLECT: I once attended a wedding where the caterer's van, loaded with all the food, was stolen prior to the reception. While the hosts scrambled behind the scenes to solve the problem, the guests waited and waited, and then began discussing how they could help. In the end, the hosts somehow found enough food and the wedding was a great success.

Perhaps a desire to help was the original motivation behind Mary's comment to her son at the wedding at Cana (v. 3). But judging from Jesus' response (v. 4), it seems she had something else in mind. She wanted everyone to know the secret she had been pondering all these years: her son was God's promised Messiah, the Savior of the world (Luke 2:19). It's only natural for a mother to want to show off her son.

But Jesus always resisted the temptation to use his power to show off (John 7:3-9). By saying, "My time has not yet come" (John 2:4), he makes clear he had a much bigger agenda in mind. Jesus had come to fulfill the mission given to him by his heavenly Father, not his earthly mother.

John adds a comment at the end of the passage to make sure his readers get the point (v. 11). Jesus performed miracles first of all because they "revealed his glory," that is, they were evidence of his divine nature. But second, they helped people, in this case his disciples, "put their faith in him." Jesus' mission was to help people believe that he was the Son of God.

So what is the significance of Jesus' first miracle? Some have said Jesus was blessing the use of wine, or that he was affirming the value of celebration. That may be part of it. But the deeper significance is far more profound. Jesus was signaling that he came to establish a new way for people to have a relationship with God, a way based not on keeping the law of Moses (that is, the complex list of rules begun with the Ten Commandments), but rather on having faith in him. Later in his ministry Jesus said this was like pouring new wine in new wineskins (Matthew 9:17). The good news is that through Jesus we can now have this new relationship with God.

APPLY: What things in your spiritual life are "old" and need to be replaced by something new from Jesus?

PRAY: Lord Jesus, I long for a deeper relationship with you. Show me how I can experience more of the new life you came to give.

57 ❧ FEAR FACTOR

PRAY: Lord, I pray that as I come to your Word today, you would use it to meet the deepest needs in my life.

READ: Mark 4:35-41

REFLECT: The facts of Mark 4:35-41 are fairly straightforward: Jesus and his disciples are in a boat when a storm blows in. Jesus commands the storm to stop, and it does. This dramatic miracle reveals another aspect of Jesus' glory: he has power over the forces of nature. That's pretty impressive.

But if I had been in that boat with the disciples, I might have felt Jesus' questions at the end were a little unfair (v. 40). "You bet we were afraid; while you were sleeping *we almost got killed!*" Anyone who's ever been out on a boat in a big storm (or even a rough sea) knows the feeling of powerlessness and fear that comes from being out of control.

Fear is something that everyone struggles with at some point. Occasionally, we may find ourselves in physical danger. But more often our fears come from pondering the endless number of worst-case scenarios that threaten us: failure at work, financial disaster, broken relationships, being alone, deteriorating health, death.

But that's the point behind Jesus' seemingly unfair questions: things are never out of control when we are with him. Once we belong to Jesus it doesn't matter what happens, it doesn't matter how bad things get. Jesus has the power to change not only the wind and the waves but also every force at work in our lives.

Of course, it would be nice to think that believing in Jesus would immediately remove all fear from our lives. But the truth is, like the disciples in the boat, we are human; we lose control and become fearful. It happens to me all the time. But that's when we need to force ourselves back to the message of this miracle: with Jesus we have nothing to fear. Faith doesn't mean that we'll never face danger or even that bad things will never happen to us. Instead, faith means believing that Jesus is in charge and knowing that we belong to him.

APPLY: What are your biggest fears? For each one, what is the root cause of the fear?

PRAY: Honestly talk to God about the things that you fear. Ask him to help you replace those fears with a surer faith in his control of your life.

58 ~ Miracle Meal

PRAY: Honestly God, sometimes I feel like I don't have the resources to solve the biggest problems in my life. Please open my eyes to your perspective on the challenges I face.

READ: Matthew 14:13-21

REFLECT: It must have been difficult at times to be a disciple of Jesus; he was constantly testing them. Sometimes he'd lead them into tough situations. Other times he'd ask them tough questions. But all the time, we get the sense that Jesus was trying to build their understanding of and faith in him. He still does that with us today.

That's what's going on in this familiar miracle: the feeding of the five thousand. Jesus already knows he can feed the five thousand men plus women and children (v. 21). But before he does, he challenges the disciples to solve the problem on their own (v. 16). What's your first instinct when you face a big problem? Do you make a plan? Do you complain? Do you go into high-energy mode? Do you become paralyzed with worry?

In this case, the disciples' first instinct was to look at their own resources (v. 17), and their conclusion was they didn't have enough to solve the problem. Not even close. But what Jesus was probing is whether or not his disciples would *look to him first* to solve the problem. Note that he says, "Bring them here to me" (v. 18). In other words, "Remember who I am; look to me first in everything that happens." It was the very same principle he taught in the Sermon on the Mount (Matthew 6:33).

I've always been curious about how Jesus did this miracle; at the critical point, the text merely says, "They all ate and were satisfied" (v. 20). I once saw a play about the life of Jesus that included this miracle. In it, the empty-handed disciples huddled with Jesus in a rugby scrum and then suddenly burst out with armloads of Italian bread. I don't know how they did that either! The point is, we don't know how or when Jesus will intervene in our lives. All we need to know is that he can, and he has resources far greater than we can ever imagine (Psalm 50:10). And that was the point of this miraculous picnic.

APPLY: What is the single biggest problem you face now? What would it mean for you to "look to Jesus first" for a solution?

PRAY: Lord Jesus, life is filled with problems. I'm just so thankful that you know my needs and you want me to come to you.

59 ❧ SEEING AND BELIEVING

PRAY: Heavenly Father, I ask that you would strengthen any areas where my faith in you is weak as I read your word today.

READ: Matthew 14:22-33

REFLECT: I once saw a television interview with an actor from the movie *The Da Vinci Code*. In response to criticism from Christians that the movie made untrue statements about Jesus, the actor said, "Well, I've always felt the Bible should include a disclaimer. A man walking on water . . ." he said squinting with one eye and tilting his head, "come on."

But just because we haven't seen something doesn't mean it couldn't be true. Peter had never seen a man walking on water either; it might have been a mirage or a ghost or something worse. Still, he stepped out of the boat. That's the essence of faith, the willingness to move forward, trusting God even when the way is unclear.

I wonder what Peter felt in that moment when he realized he was sinking into the raging waters (v. 30): embarrassment, panic, fear? Probably all of that. Now try to imagine Peter's emotions when he felt the strong grip of Jesus on his arm (v. 31). That was the moment he was sure it was no ghost (v. 26). Once Peter was safely back in the boat, there was no need to quibble about whether a man could walk on water.

I remember facing a situation that scared the daylights out of me. I was inadvertently drawn into a financial scam that threatened to wipe me out. During those days, I typed the words Jesus said to the disciples on a piece of paper and taped it next to my computer. Whenever I felt fearful, I'd look at the words and say them aloud: "Take courage! It is I. Don't be afraid" (v. 27). In so doing, I learned the lesson Peter learned from the middle of the lake: calling out to Jesus is the best way to overcome fear.

So how would you respond to the actor who wouldn't believe that Jesus walked on water? All I can say is this: I know Jesus has saved me, and I've experienced his ability to take away my fear. So it doesn't seem so unbelievable that he could also walk on water. And I don't need to see it to believe it.

APPLY: In what area of your life do you need to move forward in faith even though the way seems unclear? How could you do so?

PRAY: Spend a few minutes talking to God about that area of your life where you sense a need to step out in faith.

60 ❧ SERIOUS FRUIT

PRAY: Heavenly Father, I'd like to become a highly effective Christian. Please show me how I can do that for your glory.

READ: Matthew 21:18-22

REFLECT: It would be much easier for us to focus our attention in Matthew 21:18-22 on Jesus' encouraging comments about mountain-moving faith rather than on how he miraculously withered the poor fig tree. But the two actions are linked and were intended to teach the disciples and us some important truths.

Some might explain Jesus' outburst as a reaction to pressure; after all, the previous day at the temple had been stressful for everyone (Matthew 21:1-17). Even when they are under pressure, Christian leaders need to remember the feelings of others; they also need the understanding and forgiveness of those around them. It's hard to be perfect when you are up front all the time.

But the point of Jesus' sharp words and miraculous withering of the fig tree (Matthew 21:19) was not about relieving stress but about bearing fruit. Some commentators see the fig tree as a symbol of Israel's religion at the time; it looked good but ultimately was not satisfying the people's spiritual hunger. But it also seems to be a statement by Jesus on the urgency of his mission. He wanted his followers to know that bearing fruit is serious business and there is no time to waste.

Producing fruit involves at least two things: faith and prayer. This is something far different than "naming and claiming." It is faith built on a deep relationship with our heavenly Father and transforming prayer that enables us to understand and submit to his will—which may be radically different from our original request. But when we have waited before the Lord and honestly perceived his purposes, we can approach our "mountains" with confidence that he will move them (vv. 21-22). Jesus reminds us that the size of the tree or the height of the mountain is not a problem for God. Our challenge is developing the kind of prayer life that is built on an unwavering trust that God will accomplish his purposes, his way. As we do that, we can expect him to do incredible things in our lives.

APPLY: In what area of your life do you most need to experience mountain-moving faith? What is one step that you could take in that direction today?

PRAY: Ask God to help you bear his kind of fruit in the challenges you face today.

Discussion Questions for "The Miracles of Jesus"

1. How would you define a miracle? Do you think they are still possible today? Have you ever experienced one? Share experiences.

2. Why are people skeptical about miracles today? Do you think faith and science are compatible? How so?

3. Is there anything about the life and ministry of Jesus that seems unbelievable to you? If so, what is it and why?

4. Can you think of a time in your life when you were overwhelmed by fear? What happened and what helped you cope? Has faith in Jesus ever helped you at such times? How so?

5. Has Jesus ever miraculously provided for you? What happened?

6. When have you ever taken a big step of faith? What happened and what did you learn from the experience?

7. How would you articulate "the case for Christ"? For you, what are the strongest proofs that he was the Son of God?

More Miracles of Jesus

I DON'T BLAME PEOPLE TODAY for being skeptical about healing. I once watched a television documentary on a well-known faith healer. The cameras rolled as people from the audience were helped onto the stage. After the faith healer put his hands on them and dramatically prayed, people threw away crutches, got up out of wheel chairs or reported instant recovery from disease—all to great applause. But when the documentary followed up months later, they had trouble finding anyone who was still "healed."

Even so, most people still believe genuine healing is possible. Why? First, because suffering and sickness are so awful; in our desperation we become open to possibilities we would not be willing to consider when everything is just fine. Second, because there are many documented examples of real healing throughout history. Not only that, medical professionals today regularly report unexplained recoveries. And just about everyone knows somebody who has experienced a miraculous healing. We may not understand or agree on the reasons why, but we have to admit one thing: healing happens.

The challenge for us in the next five readings is to examine the healing miracles of Jesus with an open mind. We'll read how Jesus enabled a blind man to see, caused a disabled man to walk, restored a demon-possessed man, cured a woman with an incurable bleeding problem and brought two dead people back to life. These accounts are some of the most exciting and inspiring parts of Jesus' entire ministry.

They also give us a deeper understanding of the essential Jesus. The most basic thing we learn is that Jesus had compassion for people; he wasn't too busy or important to help people overcome their problems. Next, the healing miracles of Jesus demonstrate his power and authority, not just over sickness but also over sin. Finally, the healings provide us with more evidence that Jesus was who he said he was, the Son of God.

That's a lot to absorb all at once. So let's read through the healings one by one. As you do, try to imagine that you are there. Perhaps you could be the person receiving the healing, or one of the disciples, or even a person in the crowd. What would you have felt and said and done? Try to step into the story so you can experience the healing ministry of Jesus for yourself.

61 ᴠ Lord, I Believe

PRAY: Heavenly Father, "open my eyes that I may see wonderful things in your law" today (Psalm 119:18).

READ: John 9:1-41

REFLECT: Even a junior reporter could get the facts of the healing of the man born blind:

> JERUSALEM. An itinerant preacher from Galilee named Jesus sparked a controversy earlier today with an act of kindness. According to eyewitnesses, Jesus and his entourage met a man who had been blind from birth as they walked on the main road near Jerusalem. After a brief dialogue, Jesus put mud on the man's eyes, told him to wash in a local pond, and the man's eyesight was restored. Religious leaders have challenged the validity of the "healing" and have launched their own investigation.

Why is it so difficult for some to accept the fact the Jesus heals people? In the case of the Pharisees they were more concerned about defending a set of picky religious rules than they were about experiencing God. When told about the healing, they condemned it on a technicality (v. 16). If we ever let good things like our church traditions or our theological positions get in the way of our passion for meeting God, then something is off track.

The blind man was the only one who saw the light (v. 5). Instead of questioning or challenging Jesus, he simply obeyed (v. 7). Next, he honestly shared his experience with others (vv. 11, 25), even defending it in spite of the pressure tactics used against him (vv. 24-34). Finally, after taking time to think it through, he put his faith in Jesus (v. 38). Perhaps the strongest proof of the validity of this miracle was the fact that the blind man never backed down. He could easily have changed his story, or at least shaped it just a little, to satisfy the Pharisees and avoid "excommunication." But he didn't, he couldn't, because he could see.

The Pharisees rejected the healing because Jesus didn't fit into their religious system: "How dare you lecture us!" (v. 34). The disciples may have missed it because their interest seemed more theological than personal: "Who sinned . . . that he was born blind?" (v. 2). But the blind man was healed because he was open-minded about what Jesus could do. That's the first step to true faith, "Lord, I believe."

APPLY: Why do you think some people remain close-minded about Jesus today?

PRAY: Lord, I would like to be a bolder witness for you, like the man who was born blind. Please give me the courage to tell others how I've experienced you.

62 ✎ BAND OF BROTHERS

PRAY: Spend a few minutes talking to God about any circumstances in your life that have you feeling paralyzed either physically, emotionally or spiritually.

READ: Luke 5:17-26

REFLECT: You have to feel sorry for the poor Pharisees and the teachers of the law. They were always on the defensive. That's because Jesus was always right and in control of the circumstances, and it infuriated them. In Luke 5:17-26 I can picture these pompous religious leaders "sitting there" in the front row, arms folded, scowling as Jesus healed people (v. 17). When we find ourselves mad at God over the circumstances in our lives, we should take time to reflect on the underlying source of our anger. There may be an inconvenient truth we've been avoiding.

At the same time, you have to love the band of brothers who carried their friend to Jesus. I can imagine the hard work it took to lug a paralyzed man across town. He was heavy; it took four men to lift him. And it would have been embarrassing, "What *are* you boys doing?" But they persisted for at least two reasons. First, they loved their friend and showed it by sacrificial work. And second, they believed Jesus could make a difference. It was a simple strategy but it still works today: bring your friends to Jesus.

Now imagine the commotion and drama the crowd would have felt as the paralytic was lowered from the ceiling; it took guts and creativity to try a stunt like that. It also took faith, as Jesus pointed out (v. 20). It's significant that Jesus healed the man because of "*their* faith." Sometimes God intervenes in the lives of people based on the faith of those around them. It's a reality that should energize our prayer and service for others.

Unfortunately the grumpy old Pharisees rejected Jesus in spite of the evidence that was clear to everyone else: the paralyzed man walked out of the meeting praising God (v. 25). That's because they knew exactly what the deeper issue was: If they admitted Jesus had authority to forgive sins, they were admitting he was God (v. 21), and that was the one thing they weren't willing to do. But facing our need of forgiveness is the first step toward a restored life and relationship with God.

APPLY: In what way could you take a step of faith on behalf of someone close to you?

PRAY: Spend a few minutes asking Jesus to restore those areas of your life that need spiritual, emotional or physical healing. End with a time of praise.

63 ❧ SCARY STORY?

PRAY: Heavenly Father, as I spend time in your Word today please give me a deeper sense of your power over sin and your love for me.

READ: Mark 5:1-20

REFLECT: The reality of demon possession is difficult for modern minds to accept. It has become a popular plot line for scary movies. It's also a comic device: the cartoon image of a red-tailed alter ego sitting on someone's shoulder whispering devious thoughts always gets a laugh. But actual demon possession—that doesn't happen today, does it? From beginning to end the Bible teaches that the devil is real and that he's hell-bent on opposing God and destroying people (Genesis 3:1-15; Revelation 20:7-10).

We see a vivid example of that in Mark 5:1-20. The devil had been at work in this poor man's life for a long time. He had tortured his mind and body, and in the process alienated the man from himself and from society. Ultimately Satan wants to isolate us from God so he can destroy us (1 Peter 5:8).

But Jesus wasn't about to let that happen. First, Jesus took control of the situation and of the demons themselves (vv. 6-8). Clearly, Jesus was the higher power. Next, Jesus dealt with the demons once and for all (vv. 11-13), something the townspeople had never been able to do (v. 4). And finally, Jesus restored the man and gave him a renewed purpose in life (vv. 18-20). Often those with the darkest pasts become the most effective witnesses for God.

But this passage also contains two great ironies. First, the demons knew who Jesus really was. They almost sound like theologians, "What do you want with me, Jesus, Son of the Most High God?" (v. 7). But there's a big difference between saying all the right things about Jesus and accepting him as Savior and Lord.

The second irony is the reaction of the townspeople; instead of rejoicing, they were afraid (v. 15) and pleaded with Jesus to leave (v. 17). Maybe they thought Jesus was out to ruin their economy; two thousand pigs represented a lot of money. Or maybe they were nervous he'd come after the skeletons in their closets next. Whatever the reason, they pushed Jesus out of their lives and went back to business as usual, which is just what the devil wants.

APPLY: Is there a skeleton lurking in the closet of your heart? What will it take for you to bring this issue into the light—to Jesus?

PRAY: Pray about any unresolved issues in your past that still need healing. Also pray that God will protect you from false guilt as you do (Romans 8:1; 1 John 1:9).

64 ~ AT HIS FEET

PRAY: Lord, my life is so complicated. Sometimes I feel like I've run out of answers. All I know to do is humbly bow before you and wait for your peace and help.

READ: Mark 5:21-43

REFLECT: Politicians work hard to get "Big Mo" on their side; it's the insider's term for momentum, and it's what wins elections. Jesus was no politician, but at this point in his ministry, Big Mo was definitely working for him. His authoritative teaching and dramatic miracles were causing big crowds to follow him everywhere he went (Mark 5:21, 24). Our passage today weaves together the accounts of two miracles that occurred during this exciting and chaotic time in Jesus' ministry.

A private healing. An unnamed woman in the crowd had suffered from uncontrollable bleeding for twelve years (v. 25). Long-term physical problems often lead to emotional and spiritual depression as well. Difficult though it may be, God sometimes allows us to experience a "dark night of the soul" in order to help us see our need for him, as he did for this woman. Her friends may have criticized her desperate scheme (v. 28). But Jesus said, "Your faith has healed you" (v. 34). Sometimes faith requires us to take desperate measures.

A public healing. The daughter of a well-known synagogue ruler named Jairus, a man who would have been aligned with the group opposing Jesus, had fallen sick. But once again we see God using a health emergency to produce true faith. As Dr. C. Everett Koop, a pediatric surgeon and former Surgeon General of the United States, once said, "There are no atheists at the bedside of a dying child." His colleagues may have criticized Jairus for being a turncoat. But Jesus said, "Don't be afraid; just believe" (v. 36). Sometimes faith requires us to ignore what others think.

A common element in both of these healings is the way the unnamed woman and Jairus approached Jesus, they "fell at his feet" (vv. 22, 33). The surest way to experience Jesus' healing power is to humbly reach out to him and then wait for him to intercede in his time and in his way.

APPLY: In order to find the faith you need now, do you need to take desperate measures or ignore what others think? Why?

PRAY: Bring the area of your life where you feel the greatest sense of desperation to God in prayer.

65 ～ RESURRECTION POWER

PRAY: Lord, please help me to understand what it means to experience "the power of [Jesus'] resurrection" (Philippians 3:10-11) as I spend time with you today.

READ: John 11:1-45

REFLECT: For Jesus, raising Lazarus was a very personal demonstration of his power. Lazarus, Martha and Mary were his close friends. He had eaten with them (Luke 10:38-42), cried with them (John 11:35) and over time had come to love them deeply (John 11:3). His relationship with these siblings reminds us of a vital truth about Jesus: in addition to being the Son of God, he was also a real man. He understands what it's like to be human. He's been where we are (Hebrews 4:15).

For the religious leaders, on the other hand, this miracle was the last straw. As we've seen in previous readings, Jesus was enjoying growing popularity, and it frustrated his opponents to no end. "Eventually, though, the press will move on," they must have thought, "and we'll be back in the headlines." But when Jesus brought Lazarus back to life, the chief priests and Pharisees went over to the dark side for good (John 11:49-53). There was no way to stop someone with the power over life and death.

But that's exactly what Jesus claimed; he was "the resurrection and the life" (John 11:25-26). Instead of seeing this as a threat, his followers both then and now understand what a wonderful promise it is: believing in Jesus is the way to eternal life (John 14:6). The Bible teaches that the resurrection of Jesus was the ultimate validation of his divine nature and mission (1 Corinthians 15:1-34). This miraculous raising of Lazarus as well as the raising of Jairus's daughter were early signs of the greatest resurrection that was soon to come, when God raised his own Son, Jesus Christ, from the dead.

There's an interesting detail buried in this dramatic raising of Lazarus from death. Earlier, Martha had been the fussy complainer too distracted to be with Jesus (Luke 10:38-42). Now she's the one with time to dialogue with Jesus about the deepest truths concerning his resurrection (John 11:24). Though we've had weak moments or times of confusion about Jesus, it doesn't mean we can't keep growing in our faith. Thank God.

APPLY: A line from a popular country song says that all of us want to go to heaven but none of us want to die. How do you feel about your own death?

PRAY: Are you able to use Martha's words as your prayer? "Yes, Lord, I believe that you are the Christ, the Son of God, who has come into the world."

DISCUSSION QUESTIONS FOR "MORE MIRACLES OF JESUS"

1. Why do you think some people are skeptical about healings? What's your opinion about the possibility of healing today? Why?

2. Have you or someone close to you ever experienced what you would consider a miraculous healing? What happened?

3. How would you respond to a person who said, "Sickness is the result of sin. The first step to healing is to see if there is any unconfessed sin in your life"?

4. What's your opinion about the possibility of demon possession today? Do you think it's okay to watch movies or television programs about demon possession? Why?

5. How could you bring more of your friends to Jesus? Is that your responsibility?

6. Why is it so significant the Jesus raised Jairus's daughter and Lazarus from the dead? What did that signal to the religious leaders of that time? What does it signal to you?

7. Have you prayed to God and not been healed? How has that affected your faith?

The Prayers of Jesus

WHAT'S THE FIRST THING THAT COMES TO YOUR MIND when you think about the prayers of Jesus? Exactly! The Lord's Prayer: "Our Father who art in heaven, hallowed be thy name . . ." It's the most repeated prayer in all of human history, with the possible exception of "Lord, save me!"

Prayer is one of those things that almost everyone has tried, but almost no one fully understands. That's why our next five readings will be so helpful; they give us a picture of the greatest pray-er the world has ever known. The disciples recognized that there was something special about the way Jesus prayed. After observing him, one of the disciples spoke up for people throughout the ages when he said, "Lord, teach us to pray" (Luke 11:1). If you want to learn how to pray, watch someone who knows how to do it. And you'll find no better teacher than Jesus.

What we learn when we examine the prayers of Jesus is that he prayed in all kinds of situations and in all kinds of ways. Of course he prayed the famous model prayer for his disciples, which forms a memorable outline for anyone who wants good topics for prayer (Luke 11:1-13). He prayed spontaneous prayers when good things happened in his ministry (Luke 10:21). He prayed long formal prayers when he had far-reaching issues on his mind (John 17:1-26). And he prayed short intense prayers when he was under great pressure (Mark 14:32-42).

But as we examine these wonderful prayers, we may want to ask ourselves an important question: why did Jesus pray? After all, he was the Son of God;

he had all the power of heaven at his disposal and could do anything he wanted. The answer to that question takes us to the heart of what prayer is all about. Jesus prayed because his relationship with his heavenly Father was the most important thing to him. That's why he spent so much time talking to God, listening to God and simply spending time in God's presence.

Perhaps the greatest lesson we can learn is that Jesus didn't pray just at set times or special occasions; he prayed whenever he could (Mark 1:29-39). There's a sense in which Jesus was constantly praying; his mind and heart were always focused on his heavenly Father, and that's the essence of prayer. As you're about to discover, prayer was essential for Jesus. And if that's so, it's even more essential for us.

66 ❧ HOW DID JESUS PRAY?

PRAY: Heavenly Father, in spite of all my distractions, my heart's desire is to deepen my relationship with you. Please show me how I can grow in my ability to dialogue with you.

READ: Mark 1:29-39

REFLECT: Have you ever observed someone who is silently and intensely praying, perhaps a pastor, priest or missionary? You can't hear anything, but you can feel that something important is happening. That's the opportunity we have in this passage; we're watching the world's greatest "prayer warrior" in action, and in so doing we gain some unique insights into the prayer life of Jesus.

He prayed no matter what. Notice the context for the prayer session of Mark 1:29-39. Jesus must have been exhausted (vv. 32-34) and out of his normal routine; he was a guest in someone else's home (vv. 29-31). Those are two things that derail my prayer life.

He prayed early. Jesus got up "while it was still dark" to pray (v. 35). Prayer was the first thing on his mind for the day. What do you think about when you get out of bed?

He prayed without distraction. Jesus went to a "solitary place" to pray (v. 35). Effective prayer requires that we let go of life's distractions. Jesus prayed in spite of the well-meaning pressure from his disciples (v. 37). We'll always feel the pressure to get busy, but without prayer, it's difficult to make a difference for God.

As we read the Gospels we find other references to Jesus' pattern of prayer (Matthew 14:23; 26:36; Luke 6:12). If you sometimes feel guilty because you can't pray long, try praying more often throughout the day. You may find yourself feeling less guilty and more excited about your dialogue with God. And that's what prayer is all about.

Because Jesus' mind and heart were always focused on doing his Father's will, he was always praying: sometimes privately, sometimes formally and sometimes in the middle of the action. For us, prayer is something we make time for in the middle of our busy lives. For Jesus, interacting with his heavenly Father was the central task of his life. He made time for everything else.

APPLY: How could you make prayer less of an activity and more of a lifestyle?

PRAY: Experiment with a different approach to prayer today. For example, even if you are alone, pray aloud, try a different posture, go outside and look at the sky as you pray, take a "prayer walk" or . . .

67 ❧ THE JOY OF PRAYER

PRAY: Begin with a time of praise: "Praise the LORD, O my soul; all my inmost being, praise his holy name" (Psalm 103:1).

READ: Luke 10:1-24

REFLECT: The return of the seventy-two "missionaries" was a moment to savor. They had returned with reports of effective outreach (v. 17). You can imagine Jesus giving "high fives" to each one as they went around the circle sharing their experiences. But in the middle of this victory celebration, Jesus took time for an impromptu prayer meeting (v. 21).

The first thing we notice in this passage is the *emphasis on joy*. The missionaries were feeling the joy of success (v. 17); they had obeyed Jesus and seen results. That principle still works today. But Jesus' joy was more profound (v. 21, "through the Holy Spirit") because he saw the deeper reality to what was happening. Satan, the real enemy, was being defeated (v. 18), and God's self-revelation was becoming more clear and understandable—even to the most unlikely persons (v. 21). Too often prayer can become a solemn recitation of problems and worries. Of course God cares about those things and invites us to share our burdens with him (Psalm 68:19). But Jesus shows that when we really understand what God is doing in the world, it makes us want to shout. Joy is a vital part of prayer.

Another thing we notice in this short prayer is Jesus' *confidence in God's plan:* "Yes, Father, for this was your good pleasure" (Luke 10:21). Some people think of prayer as a kind of hopeless, wishful thinking, "Oh well, all I can do now is pray. Maybe I'll get lucky." But Jesus shows that when we really understand that God is in control of everything, we can be bold. Confidence in God's power and will is another vital part of prayer.

In spite of this inspiring prayer, Jesus knew his followers would eventually face difficulties, so he gave them some important reminders. First, no matter what happens, whether we experience success or failure, we are to live with *the kingdom end* in mind (v. 20); that puts everything else into proper perspective. And second, we are also to keep *the big picture* in mind. God has been at work for a long time (vv. 23-24) drawing people to himself, and he will continue to do so. Our responsibility is not to achieve success but to remain faithful to God, which is another reason we need to pray.

APPLY: What things about God make you feel the most joyful?

PRAY: End with a time of praise: "I will shout for joy and sing your praises, for you have redeemed me" (Psalm 71:23 NLT).

PRAY: Close your eyes and imagine that God is actually sitting with you in the room. What chair does he choose? How do you feel? What are you thinking? Now, what would you like to say to him?

READ: Luke 11:1-13

REFLECT: If someone asked you to help them develop a deeper prayer life (v. 1), how would you respond? By explaining your prayer habits, by sharing a book on the subject or perhaps by suggesting a helpful tape or seminar? Jesus begins his response by simply praying. If you want to get better at praying, he seems to say, don't spend too much time studying it. Just pray.

The Lord's Prayer (also see Matthew 6:9-15) is undoubtedly the most famous and most repeated prayer in history. Over the centuries, many of the church's best minds have analyzed this prayer. But for our purposes we can note that effective prayer involves two perspectives. First, in prayer we must *look beyond ourselves to God*, his nature, his holiness, his kingdom and his will (v. 2). And second, we should not be hesitant to *focus on our day-to-day needs*—food, forgiveness and strength to avoid temptation (vv. 3-4). Without a balance of these two perspectives, our prayers will become lopsided and eventually less effective.

After showing them how to pray, Jesus then delivers the teaching his disciples originally requested. First, he encourages boldness (vv. 5-10). Does that mean we can ask for new cars, big bank accounts and dream houses? Not exactly. Jesus' story, as well as other passages in the Bible (Matthew 6:8; 26:42; Philippians 4:19), remind us to focus on our genuine needs, not our selfish wants. The boldness Jesus encourages is related to the intensity and persistence of the requester (Luke 11:9-10), as well as the conviction that God is able to meet any genuine need.

Jesus also reflects on prayer from God's perspective, and the analogy he uses is a loving father caring for a needy child (vv. 11-13). God loves us and he knows what is truly best. Our mistake is we want to tell him what "good gift" he must give us. Sometimes we need to let go of what we think is the best solution to our problems and pray for an acceptance of his will, whatever that may be. Jesus assures us that a heart attitude of faith in our loving heavenly Father combined with a bold persistence in prayer will get incredible results (Matthew 17:20-21).

APPLY: What is one situation in your life that needs bold, persistent prayer? Is it a need or a want?

PRAY: Spend time talking to God about the biggest need in your life. Ask him to help you develop a deeper understanding of his will.

69 ❧ A DEFINING PRAYER

PRAY: Ask God for both a greater knowledge and a deeper experience of him as you spend time in his Word.

READ: John 17:1-26

REFLECT: Wouldn't you like to know what famous people prayed before their defining moment in history? For example, what did George Washington pray as he endured the long winters at Valley Forge? What did William Wilberforce pray before introducing a bill for the abolition of the slave trade in the British Parliament? What did Mother Teresa pray before starting the Missionaries of Charity in Calcutta? In John 17:1-26, we read what Jesus prayed just prior to the most significant event of his life: death on the cross.

Jesus had just given his anxious disciples their final instructions (John 13—16). He finished the session with the long prayer of John 17, which is often referred to as Jesus' "high priestly prayer," because in it he interceded for his disciples and all believers. Jesus begins, however, by praying for himself (vv. 1-5). He recognizes that "the time has come" (v. 1) for him to complete his God-given mission. For Jesus, that meant reestablishing a way for humankind to know God and have eternal life (vv. 2-3). Our God-given mission might mean any number of things, but the point is whenever we follow God's call for our lives, we bring him glory.

Jesus then prays for his disciples (vv. 6-19) and asks for three things. First, they'll need *God's protection* (vv. 11, 15). Anyone who attempts to follow Jesus will face attacks from the evil one, that is, the devil. Second, he prays that the disciples would have "*my joy*" (v. 13). He's not talking about a happy feeling. He's talking about the deep satisfaction that comes from being one with Jesus and part of what he's doing in the world. That gives us significance and reason to rejoice. Finally, he prays that they be *sanctified* (v. 19), that is, set apart or made holy, by the word of God, which is why Bible reading and prayer make such a powerful combination.

Jesus finishes by praying for everyone who would believe in him as a result of the disciples' message (vv. 20-26), and that includes you and me. His main request is for unity. Even though the institutional church has become divided and weakened over the centuries, the universal church is still one body. "That all of them may be one, Father, just as you are in me and I am in you" (v. 21). Incredible, but that's what happens when we truly believe in Jesus.

APPLY: How could you promote greater unity among the followers of Jesus you know?

PRAY: Spend some time talking to God about any defining moment that looms on the horizon of your life.

70 ❧ Pray Hard

PRAY: Heavenly Father, I'm so grateful that you are willing to accept me as your child. How wonderful to know that the all-powerful Creator of the universe knows and cares about me.

READ: Mark 14:32-42

REFLECT: Persecuted Christians around the world live in fear of a knock on the door in the middle of the night. Perhaps the most anxious moments we'll ever face are those when we know something awful is about to happen, but all we can do is wait. That's exactly how Jesus feels in Mark 14. He was "deeply distressed and troubled. . . . '[O]verwhelmed with sorrow to the point of death' " (vv. 33-34) as he waits for his accusers to show up and arrest him. I've always felt this is the most intense prayer Jesus ever prayed.

So how did Jesus pray when he was under such pressure? The answer is packed into a single verse (v. 36). He starts by simply calling out to his Father. The word *Abba* literally means "daddy." When our grandson, Noah, used to wake up in the middle of the night, he'd call out in his dark room. Even though he was scared, he knew his parents were nearby. That's how Jesus starts this prayer.

Next, he affirms what he knows to be true: all things are possible for God. It brings assurance to remember that we pray to a God who is all powerful. Jesus then makes his request; "take this cup from me," in other words, "if there's another way to accomplish your plan of salvation without sacrificing me, please do it!" There's nothing wrong with being honest with God; he welcomes that. It's hypocrisy that angers him. Jesus concludes by accepting his Father's will, whatever that may be. It was the same principle Jesus included earlier in his model prayer (Matthew 6:10).

But the intensity of Jesus' prayer is contrasted by the lethargy of the disciples' prayer (Mark 14:37-42); I wonder if Jesus was tempted to give Peter a kick. It's interesting that Jesus rebuked Peter with his old name, Simon (v. 37); the leading disciple had gone back to his old habits. But before we condemn the snoozy prayer habits of the disciples, we should admit there are times when our prayers are less than intense. There's a Christian T-shirt showing a man wearing a pair of jeans with holes in both knees. The headline simply says, "Pray hard." That's exactly what Jesus did in Gethsemane.

APPLY: Can you think of a time when you were under intense pressure? What happened to your prayer life during that time?

PRAY: Lord, you know I face situations that overwhelm me at times. But no matter what happens, my heart's cry is this: Not what I will, but what you will.

DISCUSSION QUESTIONS FOR "THE PRAYERS OF JESUS"

1. How did you first learn about prayer? Over the years, who have been your "prayer mentors" and what have they taught you?

2. How do you pray today? When do you feel that your prayers are the most meaningful and effective? Why?

3. For you, what are the most challenging or meaningful parts of the Lord's Prayer (Luke 11:1-13)? Why?

4. When you pray, do you ever experience a sense of God's presence? How does this happen?

5. Have you ever prayed for God's help in a time when you were under great pressure? What happened? How has that experience changed your view of prayers? Of God?

6. What are the biggest obstacles you face to praying? How can you overcome these?

7. How could you develop a prayer lifestyle? What are some new and creative ways you could make prayer a more significant part of your daily life?

The Hard Sayings of Jesus

IN 1742 CHARLES WESLEY WROTE THE WORDS to a hymn titled "Gentle Jesus, Meek and Mild." It thoughtfully expressed Wesley's desire to simply and completely follow Jesus. But over the years, I've heard people quote the title of that hymn as a way of expressing a rather simplistic view of Jesus: that he was some kind of sissy who walked around making fluffy moral statements that could be memorized in Sunday school or etched onto Hummel figures. Gentle Jesus, meek and mild—isn't that nice?

I hate to burst anyone's bubble, but that's not at all what Charles Wesley had in mind, and it's certainly not representative of the things Jesus said in his teaching ministry. For sure Jesus said some wonderful and encouraging things, as we've been exploring in our journey through the Bible. But as we're about to discover in our next five readings, Jesus also made many statements that were very difficult to understand. In fact, at one point in his ministry, people were so turned off by his teaching that they said, "This is a hard saying; who can listen to it?" (John 6:60 RSV), and they deserted him in droves.

Sometimes Jesus said things that were obscure; they were difficult to understand. Other times he said things that were challenging; they were difficult to obey. The five statements we'll be covering contain some from both categories:

- "Whoever eats my flesh and drinks my blood has eternal life."

- "Whoever blasphemes against the Holy Spirit will never be forgiven; he is guilty of an eternal sin."

- "You may ask me for anything in my name, and I will do it."

- "This is how my heavenly Father will treat each of you unless you forgive your brother from your heart."

- "If anyone would come after me, he must deny himself and take up his cross and follow me."

If you are intrigued by this line of study, I would suggest that you get a copy of *Hard Sayings of Jesus* by F. F. Bruce (InterVarsity Press) which covers seventy of the most challenging statements that Jesus ever made. But for now, five will do, so let's get going.

71 ✣ Soul Food

PRAY: "My soul will be satisfied as with the richest of foods; with singing lips my mouth will praise you" (Psalm 63:5).

READ: John 6:25-71

REFLECT: "Whoever eats my flesh and drinks my blood has eternal life" (v. 54).

What a strange comment! It sounds like Jesus has some wacky ideas about cannibalism. No wonder the disciples were confused and offended (vv. 60-61); their hero seems to have lost his marbles. "Couldn't you just rephrase that a little?" And no wonder the religious leaders are outraged; in addition to the disgusting image of eating human flesh, the law of Moses contained specific regulations about not consuming blood or even meat with blood in it (Leviticus 17:13-14).

But in fact this is one of the most important statements Jesus ever made. To fully understand it we must step back and look at the context. Jesus has just finished miraculously feeding thousands of people (John 6:1-15). The problem is that no one seems to understand the point of the miracle (v. 26). Most thought Jesus just liked giving out free food. Pretty cool. In fact, Jesus fed the people to demonstrate that he was the source of eternal life (v. 27). But from this point on in the dialogue, Jesus and his listeners are on two separate tracks: *they* are thinking of temporal realities (food) while *he* is thinking of spiritual realities (eternal life).

And that's the clue we need to understand what Jesus meant by his perplexing statement (vv. 53-54). He's not talking about physically eating his flesh and drinking his blood. Rather, he's talking about the spiritual union that he has with his followers. Those who truly put their faith and trust in Jesus are united with God (v. 57) and receive eternal life (v. 40). Unfortunately, the more he explains, the more divergent the separate tracks become. His listeners are looking backward to manna in the desert. Jesus is looking forward to what he would do on the cross.

Today, we have an opportunity to ponder this spiritual truth whenever we take communion. The bread and wine are reminders of Jesus' sacrifice for us and are "to be for your people the Body and Blood of your Son, the holy food of new and unending life in him" (Book of Common Prayer).

APPLY: Do you ever feel united with Jesus? When? What thoughts go through your mind as you prepare to take Communion?

PRAY: Lord, please help me draw closer to you, and please open my eyes to the spiritual realities of the world I live in.

72 ∾ A House Divided

PRAY: Lord, I don't know everything about the Bible, but I do know that it teaches about you. Please give me a better understanding of who you are as I read today.

READ: Mark 3:20-35

REFLECT: "But whoever blasphemes against the Holy Spirit will never be forgiven; he is guilty of an eternal sin" (v. 29).

When I was growing up, a common Sunday school question was, "How can I know if I've committed 'the unforgivable sin' or not?" We were afraid the Bible referred to some mysterious, unnamed offense. And worse, we worried that if we unwittingly committed it, we were doomed, with no chance of getting to heaven. The standard Sunday school answer wasn't very reassuring either: "Well, the very fact that you're worried about it shows you didn't do it." Huh?

But a careful examination of our passage today shows that the point of Jesus' statement (v. 29) was not intended to scare children. Rather, it was a sharp rebuke to the religious leaders who were accusing him of being demon-possessed (v. 30). The leaders had become frustrated with Jesus; he had been teaching, healing and attracting big crowds (v. 20). The Pharisees got so jealous they were willing to take extreme measures to protect their turf (Mark 3:6).

That's why they accused Jesus of being demon-possessed (v. 22); they wanted to discredit him in the eyes of the public. In response Jesus does two things. First, he tells a parable that easily repels the false accusation (vv. 23-27). Satan wouldn't oppose himself. Therefore Jesus' miracles couldn't be the result of demon possession. Interestingly, in 1858 Abraham Lincoln gave a famous speech titled "A House Divided," in which he made reference to this passage and used it to demonstrate the danger of dividing the United States into slave and free states.

Second, Jesus adds a zinger about eternal sin (v. 29). His point was that by equating the work of the Holy Spirit with demon possession, the religious leaders were moving 180 degrees away from God. So long as they persisted in that direction, they could not be forgiven. The truth is, the "unforgivable sin" is not some secret deed you can unwittingly commit; Jesus made it clear that he loved to forgive sinners (Luke 15:11-32). Rather, the unforgivable sin is an unwillingness to repent, an ongoing refusal to accept what Jesus freely offers, that prevents us from being forgiven.

APPLY: Over the past thirty days, have you been moving closer or farther away from God?

PRAY: Spend a few minutes confessing your sins to God. Then spend some time thanking God for the forgiveness, love and acceptance he offers through Jesus.

73 ❧ PRAYER GUARANTEE

PRAY: "Praise be to God, who has not rejected my prayer or withheld his love from me!" (Psalm 66:20).

READ: John 14:1-14

REFLECT: "You may ask me for anything in my name, and I will do it" (v. 14).

Over the years, I've heard two reactions to the puzzling statement Jesus made about prayer in this passage (v. 14). The first is "name it and claim it." According to this view, we should pray for very specific things, like a new car, a big house or a fat bank account. Isn't that what Jesus said? A friend of mine once commented how odd it is that churches who preach this prosperity gospel often have the most broken-down cars in the parking lot after the service.

The second reaction is "it ain't necessarily so." According to this view, we shouldn't pray for specific things. Often, people who feel this way claim they've tried prayer in the past, but it didn't work. But the problem with both views is they focus exclusively on earthly things, and that's a misunderstanding of what Jesus meant.

John 14:1-14 is part of a final coaching session Jesus had with his disciples (John 14—16). They've been with him for three years but now they're worried because he's talking about leaving (John 14:1-5). The disciples need some reassurance, and Jesus gives it to them in two ways. First, he says that eventually they will be with him (v. 3). Someday Jesus will return for all those who have put their faith in him as the way to God (v. 6). But second, Jesus says they can ask for his help while they wait for his return (vv. 12-14). That promise applies to you and me.

But the key to unlocking the mystery of Jesus' prayer guarantee lies in two phrases that are easy to overlook. The first is "in my name" (v. 4). When we pray, we should ask for things that are consistent with what Jesus taught and did. That narrows down my prayer list. The second is "bring glory to the Father" (v. 13). When we pray, our focus should be on things that help more people understand who God really is. Those are the kind of prayers that get results.

APPLY: What results have you seen from your prayers? How has prayer changed you?

PRAY: See if you can pray about three things that will bring glory to the Father.

74 ❧ SERIOUS FORGIVENESS

PRAY: Begin your quiet time today by praying the Lord's Prayer slowly, phrase by phrase.

READ: Matthew 18:15-35

REFLECT: "This is how my heavenly Father will treat each of you unless you forgive your brother from your heart" (v. 35).

Forgiveness is one of the toughest aspects of maintaining healthy relationships. Just ask someone who's married! But forgiveness was essential to Jesus' message and mission, and it's the theme of Matthew 18:15-35.

Jesus begins by explaining a very practical method for resolving conflict (vv. 15-20). First, talk to the person privately. Then go with others, and then involve the church. As a last resort, the relationship must be put on hold, remembering that Jesus was always willing to accept sinners who repented. Sadly, not many people have ever followed Jesus' advice. Counselors today talk about "triangulation"; that's when we talk to a third party instead of directly to the person who's offended us. It's just a fancy name for gossip, and it's deadly in a church.

In response to Jesus' forgiveness formula, Peter asks a question (v. 21) that might be restated something like this: "Lord, when is it okay to hate my brother and get revenge?" What Peter is fishing for is when he can stop forgiving. I can just imagine Jesus shaking his head and sighing, "You know, Peter, if you have to ask how many times you should forgive, you just don't get it." When we really come to understand how much God has forgiven us, there's no question that we must forgive those who offend us.

But all that sets up one of the most challenging statements Jesus ever made (v. 35). Could it really be that God gets angry with us if we don't forgive? Apparently so. Those who have been forgiven a large debt should be the most generous toward others. That's the whole point of the parable (vv. 23-34). What Jesus is saying is that our heavenly Father is serious about forgiveness, and we must be too.

APPLY: Can you think of a time when you were in the wrong and someone forgave you? How did it make you feel?

PRAY: Bring to mind one person with whom you have a broken or strained relationship. Ask God to show you what he wants you to do to make things better.

75 ✌ GET SERIOUS

PRAY: Lord, I'd love to follow you more closely. Please show me just one or two ways I can begin to do that today.

READ: Mark 8:31—9:1

REFLECT: "If anyone would come after me, he must deny himself and take up his cross and follow me" (Mark 8:34).

This passage contains one of the most misunderstood statements Jesus ever made. How many times have you heard someone moan and say in reference to some minor irritation, "Well, we all have our crosses to bear, don't we?" But for Jesus, taking up his cross was not just a coping mechanism. It was a symbol of all-out obedience to his Father's will.

But let's back up for a minute. Peter has just stumbled into one of his greatest "aha moments"; he's finally stated who Jesus really is (Mark 8:29). You'd think Peter would get a gold star for such an answer. Instead, Jesus gives a serious lecture; he teaches the disciples (v. 31) and then rebukes Peter (v. 32). Why? Because although they could now say the right things about Jesus, they still didn't understand who he was; they viewed him from a human rather than divine perspective (v. 33).

That presents a challenge for us today. Those of us who are surrounded by Christian teaching—in churches, sermons, books and radio—can quickly learn to say the right things about Jesus without understanding what it means. True understanding comes when we put into practice the things Jesus said and did. That's part of what Jesus meant by saying "follow me."

But here he links that familiar idea to an even bigger challenge—denying self and taking up a cross. For Jesus that would mean giving up his rights as the Son of God (Philippians 2:5-8) and dying on the cross for the sins of the world (John 19:17-18). For us it will mean that the focus of our lives will no longer be the pursuit of happiness. Rather it will be drawing closer to Jesus and becoming more single-minded about sharing him with others, by our words and by our actions (Mark 8:35). We must die to our own agenda and live for Jesus' agenda. In the end, that's the only thing worth living for (vv. 35-36), and the consequences of missing that point are serious indeed.

APPLY: How would you describe the focus of your life? In what ways have you taken up your cross to follow Jesus?

PRAY: Heavenly Father, I find it so easy to focus on the things of this world and so difficult to focus on the things that matter most to you. Please help me to live with your priorities today.

DISCUSSION QUESTIONS FOR "THE HARD SAYINGS OF JESUS"

1. Of all the things Jesus said (both in this section and elsewhere in the Gospels), which are the most difficult for you to understand? To obey? Why?

2. Was there ever a time in your life when you were moving 180 degrees from God? What was it like? How did you turn around?

3. Have you ever experienced a specific answer to your prayers? What happened, and how did it affect your relationship with God?

4. Have you ever failed to receive an answer to a specific prayer? What happened, and how has it affected your view of God and prayer?

5. Is it ever acceptable to hate someone? If so, when?

6. How do you usually resolve conflicts with people who have offended you?

7. Which is a bigger priority for you—pursuing happiness or following Jesus? What evidence can you offer?

The Crucifixion of Jesus

THE CROSS OF JESUS CHRIST HAS BECOME the most recognized and copied symbol in the world. Today it's a popular fashion statement whose original meaning has become lost to many people who wear or display it.

But in our next five readings, we'll go back and examine what the Bible says about the crucifixion of Jesus, and, as you'll see, it's not a pretty picture. For one thing the events that led to the death of Jesus were completely unfair and out of control, at least that's how it seemed from a human point of view. Jesus was betrayed by Judas and then deserted by all the disciples. He was arrested at night and denied any sense of due process. At the Jewish trial, the bias and hate of his accusers were obvious. And at the Roman trial, the judge knew Jesus was innocent but condemned him to die anyway.

But worst of all, crucifixion was perhaps the most gruesome form of execution ever imagined. At the time of Jesus it was used in the Roman Empire as a way of not only punishing but also humiliating enemies of the state. Victims were stripped naked, whipped to a bloody pulp and then made to carry the wooden beams on which they would be hanged. Modern medical experts suggest that death could occur from any number of causes, including shock to the body, loss of blood or simply from suffocation as the victim's body sagged and cut off the flow of air. And the process could take hours or even days to run its course. Any way you look at it, crucifixion was a horrible way to die.

One thing you'll want to keep your eye on in this section is the way Jesus reacted to the nightmare of his arrest, trials and crucifixion. Even though he was the victim, he often seemed in control of events. That's because the cross was the reason he had come to earth. He died so that all could have eternal life. He also seemed more concerned about others than he was about his own pain and suffering; especially note the things he said while he hung of the cross.

Finally, because the story of Jesus' crucifixion has been told hundreds of time in plays, movies and books, you'll want to pray about two things. First, ask God to help you see and experience these familiar passages in a fresh, new way. Second, ask God to help you understand why Jesus allowed himself to be crucified?

76 ❧ BUSTED!

PRAY: Jesus, I'm about to walk with you through the most difficult part of your life on earth. As I do, please give me a better understanding of why you did it.

READ: Matthew 26:47-56

REFLECT: Over the years scholars have speculated as to why Judas betrayed Jesus. Some say he was disillusioned: he lost faith that Jesus could ever become a political superstar for Israel. Others say he was greedy: thirty pieces of silver was an offer no thief could refuse (John 12:4-6). Still others say he was impatient: he wanted to force Jesus into action—like giving Popeye a can of spinach as the bad guys closed in.

The truth is we don't really know what motivated Judas to do what he did. What we do know is this: his act of betrayal was no accident; it was intentional. Judas planned exactly how he would stab his Master in the back (Matthew 26:48-49). But perhaps the most baffling thing about Judas's charade is that he thought he could get away with it. But don't we do the same thing today? It's no good acting as though we love Jesus while cultivating a heart full of sin (Jeremiah 17:9). Jesus saw through Judas and he sees through us.

How incredible then that Jesus still called Judas his "friend" (Matthew 26:50). Even though he knew what was about to happen, Jesus offers Judas one last opportunity to change his mind. In fact, Jesus had been giving Judas opportunities to change course throughout the Gospel accounts. The real tragedy for Judas was not this single, dramatic act of betrayal. Rather, it was the accumulation of many little acts of betrayal that led to his final rejection of the Savior.

But perhaps the most striking thing about this passage is the confidence of Jesus. Even though he could have easily stopped Judas and his posse dead in their tracks (v. 53), Jesus allows himself to be arrested without a fight; he doesn't demand to see a lawyer and he doesn't even scream for help when the rest of the disciples cut and run (v. 56). That's because his highest priority wasn't to save his own skin; it was to fulfill the mission God had given him (vv. 54, 56). He willingly gave up his life for the sins of the world (John 10:17-18).

APPLY: How do you feel when people betray you today? What does it mean to betray Jesus today?

PRAY: Lord Jesus, I'm sorry for all the little ways I turn my back on you. Please let me experience your friendship today.

77 ❧ KANGAROO COURT

PRAY: Living God, I ask you to give me a clearer understanding of Jesus "the Christ, the Son of God" as I read and pray today.

READ: Matthew 26:57-68

REFLECT: When I was a young man, I got a ticket for running a red light. Because I believed the light was yellow, I decided to appeal in traffic court. As I waited my turn to stand before the judge, I watched as, one by one, other defendants lost their appeal. Armed guards led them away to pay their fines on the spot. I suddenly had a panic attack; there was no money in my wallet, and I was at the mercy of the court.

In Matthew 26:57-68, Jesus was at the mercy of this Sanhedrin court, only the stakes were much higher. Not only that, Caiaphas and his cronies were breaking all the rules of due process. First, the trial took place at night instead of during the day. Second, the charges were based on false evidence and false witnesses (vv. 59-60). But the greatest flaw was that the judge and jury had already made up their minds; they were looking for an excuse to execute Jesus. The sad truth is, when a person makes up their mind to reject Jesus, no amount of evidence will cause them to change. Ultimately, accepting Jesus involves both a change of mind and a change of heart.

But what exactly was it that caused Caiaphas and the teachers of the law to act more like a gang of thugs than the respected leaders that they were? Actually, it was two things. First, Jesus had disrespected the temple (vv. 61-62). That's a chilling reminder not to let our religious institutions become more important than following Jesus. Second, Jesus claimed to be the Son of God (vv. 63-65); Caiaphas rightly identified that as the central issue. The problem was that he was unwilling to accept Jesus on that basis. That's the biggest mistake anyone can ever make.

I'm glad to say that when I stood before the traffic-court judge years ago, he accepted my side of the story and let me go. I left the courtroom relieved and happy. But that pales in significance to the joy I feel knowing that Jesus willingly accepted the unfair verdict of this kangaroo court so that he could pay the debt of sin for you and me.

APPLY: Have you ever had a change of mind and heart about Jesus? When and why?

PRAY: Pray for one person you know who's decided not to believe in Jesus.

78 ❧ Courtyard Debacle

PRAY: "Our God, you bless everyone whose sins you forgive and wipe away. You bless them by saying, 'You told me your sins, without trying to hide them, and now I forgive you'" (Psalm 32:1-2 CEV).

READ: Matthew 26:69—27:10

REFLECT: When I was in high school I had a good friend who was Jewish. His house contained symbols of his family's active participation in Judaism; sometimes he'd even try to teach me Hebrew phrases. One day he was visiting my house and saw symbols of our family's active participation in the Christian faith and he said, "You think the Messiah has come, but we're still waiting for him." I responded, "Well, that's where our two religions differ," and changed the subject. To this day I regret my response; it felt almost like a denial of Jesus.

But that's why this account of Peter's famous denial always gets to me; I've done it too. I'm particularly sobered by the progression of Peter's failure. His first denial is that of a double agent (Matthew 26:70); perhaps he said it just to stay inside the enemy's camp. Then, in the face of mounting pressure, he denies Jesus with greater emphasis (v. 72); it's becoming easier. When Peter is cornered and forced to declare where he stands with Jesus, he erupts with a final, angry denial (v. 74); he'd been practicing for this moment all night long.

The good news is that Jesus used this courtyard debacle to strengthen Peter's faith and empower him for a new future of productive ministry (John 21:15-19). If we are willing to repent of the ways we deny Jesus and sin against him, no failure is so great that it can separate us from God or keep us from serving him (Romans 8:28-39).

Tragically, Judas never understood that. Although he felt deep remorse (Matthew 27:3), he never came to the place of repenting. But the fact is, there was hope for him even at this final hour. Like the thief on the cross, Judas could have called out to Jesus (Luke 23:39-43) and been forgiven. Ironically, there was less hope for the chief priest and elders, whose unbelievable hypocrisy and arrogance (Matthew 27:4-10) sealed their fate.

APPLY: What are some ways you have denied Jesus? What are some ways you could stand up for him?

PRAY: Ask God to forgive you for any ways you have denied him and ask him for the courage to stand up for Jesus at the next opportunity.

79 ❧ It's All About You, Jesus

PRAY: Heavenly Father, you know the concerns of my heart today. Please guide me to the part of your Word that I most need to hear today.

READ: Luke 22:66—23:25

REFLECT: Some time ago I had lunch with two dear friends who were curious about my faith in Jesus. They asked several good, honest questions and I was encouraged by the direction of our discussion. But after a while the conversation took a turn; my friends were alarmed at the way religion and politics often mixed in public debate. As a result, they had difficulty separating my commitment to following Jesus from a particular political agenda.

That's exactly what's happening in Luke 22:66—23:25; political concerns have overwhelmed true religion. Notice the spin the religious leaders put on their accusations of Jesus: "He's undercutting our national security, he opposes your tax policy, and he's planning a political take over" (my paraphrase of Luke 23:2). It's all about politics. Thank God there are some political leaders who are attempting to govern today based on their deeply held spiritual values. But God save us from leaders who use those values for political gain. It's a fine line but an extremely important one to maintain; getting it wrong prevents people from hearing the good news.

Our passage also gives us two examples of religion and politics gone awry. Herod was interested in Jesus, but only for entertainment (v. 8); politicians always want to be near celebrities. But Jesus made clear that he was no celebrity entertainer (v. 9); we must accept him as Savior and Lord or not at all. But perhaps the most famous example came on the watch of Pilate, the man who sentenced Jesus to death. Part of him wanted to do the right thing (vv. 13-17, 20-22), but in the end he didn't believe there was any such thing as truth (John 18:38), and it caused him to reject the ultimate source of truth. Some say that is an apt analogy of our modern society.

Christians need to be very careful not to misuse faith issues in politics, or worse: to politicize the mission of the church. That's why I am moved every time I sing Matt Redman's song "The Heart of Worship" that says he's sorry for making worship about something other than Jesus.

APPLY: How have your religious beliefs shaped your political views?

PRAY: Lord, I ask that you'd reveal to me any ways my political positions are at odds with your heart and your Word.

80 ❧ REMEMBER ME

PRAY: "Remember not the sins of my youth and my rebellious ways; according to your love remember me, for you are good, O LORD" (Psalm 25:7).

READ: Luke 23:26-56

REFLECT: Whenever I read Luke 23:26-56, I have a sense that I'm on holy ground; the crucifixion of Jesus is the most amazing demonstration of sacrificial love the world has ever seen. Over the years, moviemakers have done their best to depict what it must have been like, but no one can ever fully know the extent of the suffering Jesus endured. And yet for all the physical pain, the worst part for Jesus was that God temporarily abandoned him; the Father turned his back on his beloved Son (Matthew 27:45-46). That's what it took to make a way for you and me and the entire human race to be forgiven of our sins and restored to God.

What amazes me now about this account is that even in the midst of his excruciating ordeal, Jesus was more concerned about others than himself. To the women mourning for him, Jesus offered a prophetic warning (vv. 27-31); he wanted them to be prepared for the hard times that would follow his death. To the people, leaders and soldiers who mocked him, Jesus offered forgiveness (v. 34), whether they realized they needed it or not. To the angry thief Jesus offered silence (v. 39); he didn't try to retaliate. And to the repentant thief, Jesus more than offered—he promised paradise (v. 43).

During my thirteen years on the staff of Prison Fellowship I had the opportunity to go into prison many times with its founder, Chuck Colson. Often Chuck preached to the inmates from this passage with a message that it's never too late to turn back to Jesus and accept his forgiveness for sin. Many inmates gave their lives to Christ as a result of that simple appeal.

But in a very real sense, this passage offers us a defining picture of what the essential Jesus is all about, whether we're behind bars or out in the free world. Because of our sin, all of us are condemned to die; we're either one thief or the other. The real question is, how will we respond, with insults (v. 39) or with a heartfelt "remember me" (v. 42)?

APPLY: Take time to put yourself in this story. What do you think and feel as you imagine yourself at the foot of the cross?

PRAY: Spend a few minutes humbly thanking Jesus for what he endured for you on the cross.

DISCUSSION QUESTIONS FOR "THE CRUCIFIXION OF JESUS"

1. Have you ever known, or known of, someone who has completely turned his or her back on Jesus? What caused him or her to do this?

2. Do you think some people can become so evil that they lose the opportunity to repent? Do you think Judas could have changed his mind?

3. Have you ever hidden your identity as a follower of Jesus? Why and how?

4. Have you ever been bold about your faith at a time when you felt pressure to hide it? What happened and how did you feel afterward?

5. Do you think politicians should talk about their religious beliefs? Should they govern based on their religious beliefs? Why?

6. What are the best examples today of how religion and politics should mix? How they should not mix?

7. Imagine a person who's never heard of Jesus. How would you explain the crucifixion to that person in a way he or she could understand?

The Resurrection of Jesus

EVEN PEOPLE WHO DON'T CONSIDER themselves particularly religious will often attend church services at Christmas and Easter. As a result, just about everyone knows at least two stories about Jesus, his birth and his resurrection.

What we'll do in our next five readings is cover all the major passages in the Bible about the latter story, the resurrection. First we'll look at the four Gospel accounts; you'll find it fascinating to go through them back to back. By doing so, you'll see the similarities in each account. But each Gospel writer captured different details and nuances of what happened. Matthew told his story by intertwining experiences of four people. Mark emphasizes the power that was unleashed by the resurrection. Luke adds an extended account of an encounter that two disciples had with the resurrected Jesus. And John highlights the restoration of the relationship between Peter and Jesus. It's sort of like having four reporters covering the same event. When we put all the accounts together, we get a more complete picture of what happened.

In our fifth reading, we'll look at what the apostle Paul taught about the resurrection many years after it happened. By then, the first-century Christians were beginning to have doubts about whether the resurrection of Jesus even happened, or whether it was really that important after all. So Paul wrote to reassure the doubters and to firmly reestablish the importance of the resurrection.

As you go through this section, see if you can form your own case for the resurrection from the information in the five readings. What parts of the account stand out to you? Which facts seem most convincing to you? And how could you explain your view of the resurrection to someone who wasn't sure about it?

81 ❧ RESURRECTION THRILLER

PRAY: Jesus, I want to come and see for myself what happened in that tomb. Please give me new insights into the truth about your resurrection.

READ: Matthew 28:1-20

REFLECT: I love good spy novels and thrillers; I read them in bed at night or when I'm peddling on the exercise bike at the YMCA. One of the things that appeals to me about these books is that in short chapters they often intertwine several plot lines that all come together in the end. That's exactly how Matthew constructed his account of the resurrection of Jesus.

Plot 1. The basic story (vv. 1-7). Matthew begins with a summary of the facts, told with meticulous detail. Note that the earthquake was violent (v. 2); no wonder the guards were scared stiff (v. 4). The angel had a dazzling appearance (v. 3) but assumed a casual position, sitting on the stone (v. 2). It's as if he was saying, "What's the big deal; Jesus told you this would happen, right?"

Plot 2. The two Marys (vv. 1, 5-10). The two Marys are overwhelmed with conflicting emotions, fear and joy (v. 8). Even so, the angel gives them a threefold command—don't be afraid (v. 5), come and see (v. 6), go and tell (v. 7)—good marching orders for any follower of Jesus. For the two Marys it led to a life-changing encounter with Christ (v. 9).

Plot 3. The "bad guys" (vv. 11-15). The religious leaders, aware of the disastrous public relations implications if word gets out that Jesus actually did rise from the dead, pay the guards to spread misinformation about what happened (v. 13). Sadly, there are still people today who reject Jesus because they haven't heard the truth about him.

Plot 4. The motivational conclusion (vv. 16-20). Matthew 28:18-20 is often called the Great Commission because in these verses Jesus empowered his followers to share the good news of the gospel with the whole world. But the most inspirational aspect of the Great Commission is not a vision of worldwide evangelism. Rather, it's the reality that Jesus will be with his followers forever (v. 20).

APPLY: Do you ever feel that Jesus is with you? When?

PRAY: Heavenly Father, I'm so thankful for the empty tomb. Help me to overcome my fears so I can go and tell others about your Son, Jesus.

82 ❧ GOSPEL POWER

PRAY: Heavenly Father, "I want to know Christ and the power of his resurrection" (Philippians 3:10). Show me how that's possible today as I read your Word.

READ: Mark 16:1-20

REFLECT: Perhaps your Bible includes a note indicating that most early manuscripts don't include Mark 16:9-20. What's that all about? Over the years, scholars have offered different explanations, but the most likely is that either Mark died just before he finished his Gospel account or the last section of his scroll was somehow destroyed, and as a result, someone close to Mark filled in the last section. We'll never know for sure. Still, these verses are included because they help fill in the picture of this exciting time.

So what do we learn from Mark's account of the resurrection? First, we note the many similarities to other Gospel accounts, a fact that enhances the credibility of this passage. Mark reports that the resurrection was discovered early on the "first day of the week" (Sunday) by the women close to Jesus (v. 2), and that an angel (described as a young man) was present to explain things (v. 5). And note that the angel's message is virtually the same as we read in Matthew (compare Matthew 28:5-7 with Mark 16:6-7). Everyone has the same basic story.

But our reading today gives us two unique insights into this momentous day.

There are consequences to our choices about the gospel (vv. 15-16). In this version of the events around the resurrection, Jesus' words are not just a motivational challenge, "Go into all the world" (v. 15). Here, they are linked to another of his "hard sayings"; our response to the good news determines whether we're "saved" or "condemned" (v. 16). We must be very careful not to scare or manipulate people with these words. But on the other hand, it's important to know there are consequences to our decision about Jesus.

There is power in the message of the gospel (vv. 17-18). You may not feel comfortable with all the examples listed here; personally, I'm not a big fan of snakes. Again, we must be careful with these verses; we shouldn't sensationalize them or attempt dangerous things without clear direction from the Lord. But the fact remains Jesus said we would do "even greater things" after his death and resurrection (John 14:12). That's a powerful message.

APPLY: For you, what is the most powerful thing about the resurrection of Jesus? Why?

PRAY: Spend a few minutes asking God to show you how you could respond to the Great Commission in your world.

83 ❧ THE THIRD DISCIPLE

PRAY: Heavenly Father, I thank you that "your word is truth" (John 17:17). I pray that you will open my eyes to clearly see and understand more of that truth today.

READ: Luke 24:1-49

REFLECT: Some people enjoy looking for "inconsistencies" in the Bible. For example, Matthew reports there was one angel at the empty tomb while Mark saw a "young man." Luke says two men were present while John says there were two angels. Are these true inconsistencies? Hardly. What's clear from all the descriptions is that these were angelic beings. And it's perfectly reasonable to think that at times there was one or two present. Hyperventilating over the details of the resurrection accounts can cause us to lose sight of the main point: Jesus was no longer in the tomb.

The unique feature of Luke's account is the report of Jesus' appearance to the two disciples on the road to Emmaus (vv. 13-35). We can easily imagine the shock and discouragement these men were feeling (v. 17). For the past three years they'd been on a wild ride with Jesus as he preached the good news, healed the sick and confronted the religious leaders. The problem was they didn't understand who Jesus really was; they thought he was a prophet destined to become Israel's political savior (vv. 19-21). So when he died, they concluded it was "game over" for Jesus and for Israel.

We can also feel the frustration in Jesus' response, which was in essence, "Guys, you've missed the whole point!" (v. 25). Jesus wasn't the leader of a political movement; people still have that misconception today. He was "the Christ," the one God had promised to send in order to save humankind from sin (v. 26). And the way he would accomplish that is through suffering, death and resurrection.

Wouldn't you love to have been part of this private Bible study with Jesus? In a sense, you are. As you discover for yourself "what was said in all the Scriptures" (v. 27) about the essential Jesus, it's as if you are "the third disciple" on the road to Emmaus. And my prayer is that you'll come to the same conclusion as the others: "It is true!" (v. 34).

APPLY: What misconceptions about Jesus do people seem to have today? What could you do to share the truth about Jesus?

PRAY: Pray for one person you know who is confused about who Jesus really is.

84 ❧ FOLLOW ME!

PRAY: Prayerfully think of the pressures and stresses you face today. Imagine that you are handing each one to Jesus so you can be free to rest with him.

READ: John 20:1—21:25

REFLECT: There are many good ways to get a better understanding of the Bible's message. One way is to develop a daily quiet time, that is, to prayerfully read a short Bible passage each day and then reflect on how to live it out. Another is to read through the Bible in a year; another is to conduct an in-depth study of a single book of the Bible. Our reading today presents us with yet another option: character studies. John reports on the resurrection of Jesus by describing how different people reacted to this significant event.

Mary Magdalene was a woman whom Jesus had cured of demon-possession (Mark 16:9; Luke 8:2). All the Gospel accounts report she was the first one to the tomb that morning. Often a person who has been forgiven the most will become the most committed follower of Jesus.

Thomas will forever be remembered for his doubts. But I believe he also deserves credit for his honesty. Others had questions about Jesus' resurrection (John 20:9), but Thomas was the only one with the guts to admit them—and to publicly change his mind when presented with the truth (John 20:28).

Peter, one of the disciples Jesus had groomed for leadership (Matthew 17:1; Mark 14:33; Luke 8:51), had failed Jesus big-time in his hour of need (Matthew 26:69-75). It's significant that in John 21:15-19 Peter must reaffirm his love for Jesus three times, matching his three denials. Once their relationship is restored Jesus takes Peter back to the very first words he ever said to him, "Follow me" (John 21:19; Matthew 4:19). It's as if Jesus is saying, "Look, if you want to be a leader, you must first understand what it means to be my follower."

John is the fourth character in this passage. Although he tries not to attract attention, it's clear he has developed a special relationship with Jesus (John 20:2; 21:7, 20-24), and a firm belief in the truth of his resurrection (John 20:8). The two go hand in hand.

APPLY: Which of the four characters in this passage do you identify with the most? Why?

PRAY: Lord, I admit that I have doubts and failures. But even so, my greatest desire is to be your committed follower. Show me how to do that today.

85 ❧ FACT AND HOPE

PRAY: Heavenly Father, as I read and reflect on these words today, I ask that you give me a deeper experience of the living Jesus.

READ: 1 Corinthians 15:1-58

REFLECT: Our reading today is part of a letter written by the apostle Paul to the church in a first-century city named Corinth. It had been several years since Jesus lived, and people were beginning to ask tough questions: Did his resurrection actually happen? Does it really matter if it did or didn't? And if it did, what significance does it have for us now? When you think about it, these are the same questions people have today.

So how did Paul answer? He starts by giving his account of the resurrection (vv. 3-8), which includes all the facts we discovered in the four Gospels. Although Paul didn't go to the empty tomb himself that morning, he did have an encounter with the resurrected Jesus some time later (Acts 9:1-19). He also had another reliable source of information, one that is still available to us today: he studied the Scriptures (vv. 3-4). That's the best way to answer our questions about Jesus. Here, Paul addresses two key issues:

The historical fact of the resurrection (vv. 12-34). The historicity of the resurrection is still a big issue today. Some want to deconstruct the Bible; others want to reinterpret what it says: "Well, whether the tomb was empty or not isn't important. Just the idea of new life is inspirational." "Baloney!" Paul would shout in response. Jesus was actually raised from the dead (v. 20), and there were lots of eyewitnesses (vv. 5-8). Saying it didn't happen isn't inspirational; it's untrue and undermining of our entire faith (vv. 17-19). So knock it off!

The personal impact of the resurrection (vv. 35-58). In different ways, the Corinthians were asking, "Okay, if there is such a thing as resurrection from the dead, how will it affect me?" Paul does his best to describe our resurrection bodies (vv. 37-49), but as he said earlier, "now we see but a poor reflection" (1 Corinthians 13:12); we won't really know what it will be like until it happens. What we do know is that our spiritual bodies will be imperishable, glorious and powerful (vv. 42-44). That gives us a lot of hope; but it is a hope based on the fact of the resurrection (1 Peter 1:3).

APPLY: For you, what facts make the strongest case for the resurrection of Jesus?

PRAY: Heavenly Father, I ask that you increase my faith and hope in the fact of the resurrection of your Son, Jesus.

DISCUSSION QUESTIONS FOR "THE RESURRECTION OF JESUS"

1. What was your reaction the first time you heard about the resurrection of Jesus? How has your understanding changed over the years?

2. How would you respond to a church leader who said, "You can still be a good Christian and not believe that Jesus was literally raised from the dead. It just doesn't square with what we know about science today"?

3. For you, what are the three most convincing proofs of the resurrection?

4. Have you ever had a major misunderstanding about something in the Bible? What was it? How can you know if your interpretation of the Bible is correct?

5. Based on Jesus' response to Peter, how should we respond to those in church leadership today who have had a major failing?

6. Do you have any lingering questions about the resurrection of Jesus? What are they, and what answer does the Bible give to them?

7. How are you responding to the Great Commission Jesus gave his followers? How do you share the good news about Jesus in your world?

The Early Church of Jesus

WHEN MY FAMILY AND I MOVED BACK TO PENNSYLVANIA several years ago, we had to find a new church. For about a year we visited various congregations near our home. This gave us an opportunity to participate in a variety of Christian traditions and worship styles. I was encouraged to discover that there were many Christ-centered churches in our area.

But our search for a new church home also gave us a feel for the unique dynamics within each one. One church had a large endowment but a small congregation and no full-time pastor. Another church had a great preacher with many full services on Sunday and lots of programming throughout the week, but it was such a busy place that we found it hard to connect with anyone. Still another church had a familiar liturgy, but the people seemed uninterested, as if they were just going through the motions.

Our next section covers the first three chapters in the book of Revelation, which is the record of a vision the apostle John had nearly sixty years after the death and resurrection of Jesus Christ. In the vision it's as if Jesus himself has been a newcomer in seven first-century churches, and he describes the unique dynamics within each one. Imagine what Jesus would say if he visited your church next Sunday!

Of the seven churches mentioned in Revelation, five fall into a "good news–bad news" category; Jesus commends them for some things but scolds them for others. Only two of the churches fall into an "all good" category; Jesus praises them in spite of the fact that they are both facing severe struggles.

As you'll discover, some of the details in the book of Revelation are difficult to understand. That's because it's the record of a vision, and like a dream that you have at night, it's the main point that you ponder in the morning. And the main point of the next five readings is this: Jesus knows what's going on in the church, and he really cares about it. So let's get going and see if we can piece together what Jesus thinks about *his* church.

86 ⌣ A VISION FOR THE EMERGENT CHURCH

PRAY: Heavenly Father, I ask that you would give me a clearer vision of your Son, Jesus Christ, as I read and pray today.

READ: Revelation 1:1-20

REFLECT: People sometimes refer to the last book of the Bible as "John's Revelation." But that's a little misleading because it is actually "the revelation of Jesus Christ" (v. 1), as the opening sentence makes clear. What we need to understand as we begin our exploration of this challenging book is that although the apostle John recorded this incredible vision, the book of Revelation is all about Jesus.

And right away we notice the consistency between John's perspective and the rest of the New Testament. Jesus is "the firstborn from the dead" (v. 5; Colossians 1:15, 18); he has freed us from sin "by his blood" (v. 5; Romans 5:9; Ephesians 1:7); his followers are "a kingdom and priests" (v. 6; 1 Peter 2:9); and someday Jesus will come again and "every eye will see him" (v. 7; Philippians 2:9-11).

But John also gives us plenty of new information about Jesus. The first thing we notice is his majestic appearance and powerful voice (vv. 12-15). When Jesus was on earth, John got as close to him as anyone. But in the vision of Revelation 1, John sees Jesus in all his heavenly glory. That contrast only highlights the miracle of the incarnation; in Jesus the God of the universe became one of us. The second thing we notice is Jesus' description of himself: he is eternal, he is alive, and he will decide who goes to heaven or hell (Revelation 1:17-18). That's why we must take our decision about him very seriously. It will have eternal consequences.

But the last thing that stands out in this passage is that Jesus has something to say about the emergent church of the first century (v. 11). It reminds us that he knows and cares what goes on in our churches too, which is a sobering thought. But the church is not a building; it is a body. Jesus cares so passionately about the church because he is one with it (John 17:20-21).

APPLY: How do you view Jesus: as majestic and powerful or close and friendly? Why?

PRAY: Spend a few minutes thanking Jesus for the things you learned about him in this passage.

87 ✤ UNFAITHFUL OR FAITHFUL?

PRAY: Lord, there are lots of things that get in the way of my love for you. Help me to start over with you today as I read your Word.

READ: Revelation 2:1-11

REFLECT: Throughout my adult life I've been a member of three different churches, depending on where I worked and lived. As I think back, I realize each one was different. Some had strong teaching, some didn't. Some were active in the community, some weren't. Some had lots of people and resources, some didn't. For a variety of reasons they all had their strengths and weaknesses. That's the sense we'll get as we read Jesus' assessment of the churches in the first century.

The first church that comes up for review was in the city of Ephesus (vv. 1-7). The good news about this body of believers is that they were activists; they were willing to work hard (v. 2). Not only that, they were careful to avoid false teaching and even suffered for their beliefs. The bad news was they'd forsaken their first love, Jesus (v. 4). They were like a husband who provides everything his family needs but who is unfaithful to his wife. If there's not true love for Jesus in the church, its members are just going through the motions, and Jesus doesn't like that. The way to rekindle dying love is to repent and start over again (v. 5).

The second church, Smyrna (vv. 8-11), was one of two that were singled out for commendation only. (The other is in Philadelphia [Revelation 3:7-14].) But to the casual observer the church in Smyrna may have looked like a failure. They were poor, they were being criticized, and their members were about to suffer persecution and imprisonment (vv. 8-10). That's not such a great formula for church growth. Or is it?

Today, the churches around the world that are facing the greatest persecution are also experiencing the fastest growth. That doesn't mean we should throw our own churches into turmoil in an effort to boost attendance. But it reminds us that when Christians stand strong for the gospel, as they must in persecution, the church will attract people. Jesus calls that faithfulness (v. 10), and that's what he wants to see in his church.

APPLY: What would it mean for your to stand strong for the gospel this week?

PRAY: Spend a few minutes praying for the churches you've been part of or come into contact with in your life.

88 ∾ HOLD ON—UNTIL I COME

PRAY: Thank God for all the ways your involvement in the church has helped you grow closer to him and to others.

READ: Revelation 2:12-29

REFLECT: I know people who have been searching for the perfect church all their lives. They evaluate (and criticize) the pastor, preaching and programs wherever they attend, and then move on. It's important to find a church that loves Jesus and believes the Bible, and that may take some looking. But as Groucho Marx once said, "I refuse to join any club that would have me as a member." Churches aren't perfect because they're made up of imperfect members.

The two churches in Revelation 2:12-29 certainly weren't perfect; in fact, they had the same basic problem. The church at Pergamum (vv. 12-17) had a wonderful history: they had remained true to Jesus during a period of unusual stress and persecution (v. 13). But that spiritual victory was long past; now they were being enticed by false teaching (vv. 14-15). There are churches and denominations today who have a wonderful history of evangelism and outreach but who have lost their commitment to the gospel and biblical teaching. As a result, they are gradually dying. Jesus says the way to fix that situation is straightforward: "Repent!" (v. 16).

The members of the church in Thyatira (vv. 18-29) also had some good points; they were a loving, faithful, serving and persevering congregation (v. 19). What pastor wouldn't be happy with that? But the church in Thyatira had the same problem as Pergamum: they were tolerating false teaching, and notice that it led to immoral behavior (v. 20). When human reason takes a higher place than biblical principles, the church begins to look no different than the world. A recent survey found that born-again Christians were just as likely to divorce as non-Christians, for example.

But all this raises an important question: how do we live with the fact that there's no perfect church? Jesus says, "Hold on to what you have until I come" (v. 25). In other words, remain faithful to the gospel and God's Word, and eagerly look forward to his return. We can do that no matter what church we belong to.

APPLY: What false teaching have you encountered over the years? Did any of it entice you? Why?

PRAY: Lord, you know the church isn't perfect and neither am I. Even so, help me to hold firmly to the gospel and to look eagerly for your return.

89 ∾ THE DEAD CHURCH

PRAY: Heavenly Father, I want to be "dead to sin" but "alive to God" (Romans 6:11). Please show me how I can do that today.

READ: Revelation 3:1-13

REFLECT: Years ago I attended an urban church that some of my friends thought was dead. It was part of a denomination that was drifting away from the Bible. The church was located in a transitional neighborhood, and we struggled to maintain a large stone building that hadn't been filled in fifty years. But a small group of us began meeting in a side chapel once each week to pray for the church. As a result, God did a wonderful thing: he didn't suddenly fill the pews, but he made those of us who prayed spiritually alive.

The church in Sardis (vv. 1-6) was the reverse of that urban church I attended. It had "a reputation of being alive" (v. 1). Today, everyone wants to be part of a successful church. Megachurches attract the best preachers, the most money and the largest congregations. But is that what Jesus wants? Not necessarily.

Even though the church in Sardis had everything going for it, Jesus considered it dead (v. 1). Why? Because its members weren't fully obeying the basic teachings of the gospel (vv. 2-3). That can happen if we focus on a few "precious promises" but aren't committed to reading and applying all parts of the Bible. Without that, Jesus says to the church in Sardis, "you are not completely obeying God" (v. 2 CEV).

The church in Philadelphia, on the other hand, received only kudos (vv. 7-13). Like the church at Smyrna, they didn't look successful; they were weak and facing opposition (vv. 8-9). But they got the main things right; Jesus says, "You obeyed my word and did not deny me" (v. 8 NLT).

Perhaps the most encouraging thing from this passage is that whether you find yourself in a dead church or one that is truly alive, Jesus says you will "walk with me" (v. 4) if you remain faithful to him and his Word. The best reason to read and live out the full message of the Bible is not so that we can be "holier than thou"; it's so that we can be closer to Jesus.

APPLY: Do you think Jesus would consider your church dead or alive? Why?

PRAY: Spend this time praying for the church you attend and for all the churches near where you live.

90 ❧ LUKEWARM FOR GOD

PRAY: "Praise be to God, who has not rejected my prayer or withheld his love from me!" (Psalm 66:20).

READ: Revelation 3:14-22

REFLECT: People who are passionate about God today are often labeled "extremists." A society that worships a valueless form of tolerance is threatened by anyone who knows what they believe and is willing to talk about it. Of course, we shouldn't try to cram our beliefs down the throats of others; that does more harm than good. But there's nothing wrong with making God our first priority; that's what he wants (Matthew 6:33).

No one would ever accuse the church in Laodicea (vv. 14-22) of being a bunch of religious extremists; they were lukewarm for God, and that really bothered Jesus (vv. 15-16). It still does. For the Laodiceans, it was their wealth that had dulled their passion for the things of God (v. 17). Those of us who have material possessions should be thankful for what we have, but we should also heed this warning to the Laodiceans; it's impossible to love both God and money (Matthew 6:24). It's like trying to marry two people at the same time; it just doesn't work.

There are two other ideas in this passage worth pondering. The first is the connection between discipline and love (v. 19). Sometimes we may think that when bad things happen, God is out to get us. That may be so, but he's out to get us to repent, as Jesus makes clear (v. 19). The fact is, God has an extreme love for us, so much so that he sent his Son to die for our sins (John 3:16; 1 John 4:9).

The second idea is really a word picture that communicates how much Jesus wants to be with us (v. 20). When I was growing up, it seemed like every Sunday school classroom in the world had the same picture of a fair-haired Jesus knocking on a door in some garden. Those pictures may have been a little schmaltzy, but they communicated an important truth to me: Jesus is waiting for me to invite him into my life.

APPLY: How would you characterize your relationship with Jesus right now—on fire, on ice or lukewarm? Why?

PRAY: Pray about one way you could show your love for God this week, no matter what people think about you.

DISCUSSION QUESTIONS FOR "THE EARLY CHURCH OF JESUS"

1. If Jesus came to your church, what do you think he'd say? What message might Jesus have for the churches in your country?

2. Is it a good thing that, in general, the church of the West doesn't face persecution? How can a congregation remain faithful when they live in peace and prosperity?

3. How can a church that's become large, wealthy and powerful keep Jesus as its first love? Do you know of any examples?

4. How can a person who's become successful keep Jesus as his or her first love? Do you know of any examples?

5. Do you think Christians today have become too tolerant or too extreme? Why?

6. If you find yourself in a dead church, how can you know when it's time to move to a new church or to stay and try to make things better? Have

you ever been in this situation? What happened?

7. Have you ever felt lukewarm in your relationship with God? Have you ever been in a church that felt that way? What could you do to help your church "stay awake"?

The Second Coming of Jesus

THE BIBLE TELLS US THAT AS JESUS was ascending into heaven after his death and resurrection, two angels appeared and said to the disciples, "This same Jesus, who has been taken from you into heaven, will come back in the same way you have seen him go into heaven" (Acts 1:11). Ever since, the second coming of Jesus has been eagerly anticipated by his followers in every age.

As early as the first century, however, questions began to emerge. Some people thought that the second coming had already occurred and that they had been left behind. Others thought that it would never happen and they mocked Christians who were still waiting. Still others used the confusion over the second coming to teach their own kooky views of the end of the world. What's ironic is that all those things are still happening today.

That's why our next five readings are so useful; they'll help us clarify what the Bible says about this important topic. We'll begin by examining the ascension of Jesus; it's a preview of what his second coming will be like. Then we'll dig into the teachings of two key leaders in the early church—Paul and Peter—to find out how they answered the questions that were being raised. And finally, we'll take a look at Revelation 21—22, the last two chapters of the Bible, to get a picture of what the end times will be like. And the encouraging thing is that the end is only the beginning of a new world with God at its center.

But if the Bible is so clear about the second coming, why do so many still seem confused about it today? The answer, I believe, is that people take the information in the Bible to one of two extremes. Some make too much of the second coming; their whole worldview is built around the most obscure details of the end times. Others make too little of the second coming; for them, it might happen, it might not, but who cares?

That's why our goal in this section will be to form a balanced, biblical view of the second coming. Because the one thing that is beyond question is that some day Jesus will come back in the same way that he went up into heaven. What a joyous day that will be!

91 ❧ THE GREATEST SEQUEL OF ALL TIME

PRAY: Lord, I ask that you would send the Holy Spirit to "guide me into all truth" about your death, resurrection, ascension and second coming.

READ: Acts 1:1-11

REFLECT: Have you ever watched a movie that leaves you feeling that a sequel is coming? Perhaps the bad guy has been defeated but is still lurking out there somewhere. Or maybe the good guy has overcome his present struggles and is now ready for a new adventure. In a sense, that's exactly what's happening in this passage. Luke, the writer of Acts, is setting up the greatest sequel of all time; he's preparing us for the second coming of Jesus Christ.

He does that by describing the dramatic conclusion to Jesus' life on earth. Luke had finished his Gospel account with a reference to the ascension of Jesus (Luke 24:50-53), but here he gives a fuller description of that unforgettable event. Note that he makes a point of reviewing the growing body of evidence for Jesus' resurrection (v. 3). There were many eyewitnesses.

But for some, seeing is not always believing. Even after all the "convincing proofs" (v. 3) the disciples had witnessed, they still hadn't grasped the truth about Jesus. They couldn't get over their assumption that he was Israel's national hero (v. 6). All of us bring assumptions to our consideration of Jesus, some accurate and some not. One of the best ways to get a true picture of the essential Jesus today is to prayerfully read what the Bible says about him.

Another way is to rely on the Holy Spirit. Earlier Jesus taught that the Holy Spirit would help his disciples understand the truth of the gospel after his death, resurrection and ascension (John 16:13). Now Jesus says the Holy Spirit will give his followers power for sharing that truth with a needy world (Acts 1:8). Through the Holy Spirit, we can be effective witnesses both by our words and by our actions.

But as Jesus disappears into the clouds, it is the two angels who have the privilege of announcing the great sequel. Jesus "will come back in the same way you have seen him go into heaven" (v. 11). Just imagine what that would be like if it happened today!

APPLY: If you knew Jesus was returning within the next thirty days, what difference would it make for your plans and priorities?

PRAY: Lord, I can hardly imagine what it will be like when you return. All I know is that I'm so thankful that you've made a way for me to be with you forever.

92 ⊸ IF I SHOULD DIE BEFORE I WAKE

PRAY: Heavenly Father, "keep us in [your] grace, and guide us when perplexed; And free us from all ills, in this world and the next" (Martin Rinkart).

READ: 1 Thessalonians 4:13—5:11

REFLECT: I read the newspaper almost every morning, and I have a pattern for how I go about it. First I look at the front page, then sports, then news and editorials, then celebrity gossip, and finally the obituaries. For some reason I'm always curious about who died. (Admit it, you are too!) People throughout the ages have been intrigued by this question: what happens to me after I die? That's exactly the question the believers in the first-century city of Thessalonica were pondering, and 1 Thessalonians 4:13—5:11 is the apostle Paul's answer to them.

Paul starts by reviewing the basic teaching of the gospel on this subject: those who believe that Jesus died and rose again can be certain that they'll enjoy eternal life with him (1 Thessalonians 4:14, 17). Paul then offers a succinct description of what Jesus' return will be like (1 Thessalonians 4:16); it's a description that sounds very similar to others in the New Testament because it's based on the explanation Jesus himself gave (1 Thessalonians 4:15; Matthew 24:1-51).

Paul then gives the Thessalonians two practical teachings to help them maintain a balanced understanding of the second coming. First, they *shouldn't* spend time trying to nail down the exact "times and dates" (1 Thessalonians 5:1-3); people are still distracted by that debate today, and the truth is that only God knows when it will happen (Matthew 24:36). What we do know is that if we're not prepared, Jesus' return will take us by surprise. It will be like a "thief in the night" (1 Thessalonians 5:2).

Second, Paul teaches that they *should* spend time trying to live for God in the present (1 Thessalonians 5:4-8). That's good advice for us too. We are to put off the deeds of darkness and put on the lifestyle of those who live in the light, which sounds exactly like the advice Paul gave to the believers in Ephesus (Ephesians 4:20-24; 6:10-18). We'll always be curious about the second coming. But Paul reminds that the most important thing to know is simply that we are ready for it.

APPLY: What is your answer to the question, "What will happen to me after I die?"

PRAY: Spend some time praying about the ways you could become more ready for the return of Jesus Christ.

93 ∿ DON'T BE ALARMED

PRAY: "Be exalted, O God, above the heavens; let your glory be over all the earth" (Psalm 57:11).

READ: 2 Thessalonians 2:1-12

REFLECT: Recently I was given a book written by a Christian author with whom I was unfamiliar. The first thing I did was look at the back cover to see the list of his other books. I was surprised to learn that one of his previous bestsellers was described as "the definitive book on the afterlife." Really? I thought *that* book was written a long time ago. It's called the Bible, and our reading today gives us another puzzle piece for the picture of the second coming we've been forming from it.

The first thing we learn from Paul's second letter to the Thessalonians is that some people were sensationalizing the second coming, or simply spreading misinformation about it. As a result, many believers worried they had been left behind (v. 2). Paul says "don't let anyone deceive you" (v. 3), and he proceeds to remind them of the basics: When Jesus returns, his followers will be with him (v. 1). In other words, when it happens, you'll know.

But as Paul continues, he gives us some new information about the end times. In particular, the trigger events will be some kind of "rebellion" and the appearance of "the man of lawlessness" (v. 3). What in the world is he talking about? In different places throughout the Bible we find references to a final showdown between God and Satan; that's the rebellion. Also during that final conflict a key instrument of Satan, called the antichrist, will oppose God and be defeated (Matthew 24:1-51; Mark 13:1-37; Revelation 19:19-21; 20:7-10). Although Paul doesn't take time in this letter to explain everything, that's clearly what he has in mind.

So what does all this mean for us today? Simply this: We shouldn't become "unsettled or alarmed" (v. 2) if world events seem out of control. The Bible teaches that God will let things get worse before he steps in to fix it once and for all. But remember; we've already peeked at the end of the story; Jesus is coming back, and that's all we really need to know.

APPLY: How does your understanding of the second coming of Jesus affect the way you react to world news today? Why?

PRAY: Lord, this world would be a really scary place if I wasn't sure that you were coming back someday. Please show me how I can serve you best until that day.

94 ᴠ Waiting for . . . ?

PRAY: Heavenly Father, when it comes to the second coming, I sometimes feel like this: "I do believe; help me overcome my unbelief!" (Mark 9:24).

READ: 2 Peter 3:1-18

REFLECT: I once saw a college production of *Waiting for Godot*, the famous play by Samuel Beckett about two tramps, Vladimir and Estragon, who spend the entire play anticipating the arrival of a person named Godot. They talk, they have conflict, they meet other characters, but in the end Godot never shows up. Although Beckett refused to explain the play, his message was clear: life is meaningless if we spend it waiting for something that never happens.

That's exactly how some first-century Christians were beginning to feel about the second coming of Christ. They were waiting, waiting, waiting, but nothing was happening. And to make matters worse, skeptics were becoming more vocal with their taunts (v. 4). Today, it's over two thousand years later, and Jesus still hasn't returned. Have Christians been suckered into some meaningless play with Vladimir and Estragon? "Absolutely not!" is how the apostle Peter would answer, and he devotes the last section of 2 Peter to explaining why.

The biblical response. First he points to the words of the prophets and the words of Jesus himself (v. 2). Even though it's centuries later, we have access to both in the Bible. But the reality is, people have always doubted

God's Word. So Peter reminds his readers that when God speaks, things happen, like at creation and at the great flood in the time of Noah (vv. 5-6). And since God's Word says the second coming will happen, we can be sure it will (v. 7).

The philosophical response. God is outside of time (v. 8); he doesn't sit around marking his calendar like we do. As a result, what seems like a long delay is actually a big opportunity for more people to come to know him (v. 15).

How should we then live as we wait for Jesus to return? We should focus on living "holy and godly lives" (v. 11). Then we'll be drawing closer and closer to Jesus while we wait for that day when we meet him face to face (1 Corinthians 13:12).

APPLY: Do you ever have doubts about the second coming of Jesus? What are they, and what helps you overcome them?

PRAY: Lord, I ask for your help to live a holy and godly life while I wait to meet you face to face someday.

95 ❧ ONLY THE BEGINNING

PRAY: Heavenly Father, as I near the end of my journey through the Bible, help me to get a clear understanding of the essential Jesus.

READ: Revelation 21:1—22:21

REFLECT: When I start reading a novel, I often turn to the back and scan the last few paragraphs first. Some people think that ruins all the fun, but I like to find out who will be left standing by the end of the story (shows you what kind of books I read!). But in a sense, that's what we are doing in our passage today; we're reading the last paragraphs of the Bible, and they give us a glimpse of the greatest happily-ever-after conclusion we could imagine.

As we discovered in our last section, the book of Revelation is a vision that the apostle John had several decades after the resurrection (Revelation 1:9-10). In Revelation 1—3 the focus was on specific messages from Jesus to seven first-century churches. But in Revelation 21—22 the focus has switched to the end of the world, and we discover that God intends to establish "a new heaven and a new earth" (21:1). That's an encouraging thought when we consider what's happening in the world today.

There are probably a few things about this passage that you found difficult to follow. What we need to remember is that Revelation is the record of a vision; it's best to focus on the main point rather than every little detail (see p. 171 in "The Early Church of Jesus").

And the main point is very clear. In the end Satan will be defeated (Revelation 20:7-10), the curse of sin will be broken (Revelation 22:3), and the Father and Son will be present with us. "God's home is now among his people! He will live with them, and they will be his people. God himself will be with them" (Revelation 21:3 NLT). What an incredible vision that is!

For those who belong to Christ, the end of the world is only the beginning of eternal life (Romans 6:23). That's the Bible's greatest story, and that's the heart of the essential Jesus story.

APPLY: How does God's plan to establish a new heaven and a new earth affect the way you live now?

PRAY: Lord, I look forward to the day when I'll see your face. Help me to live my life with that end in mind. Come, Lord Jesus.

DISCUSSION QUESTIONS FOR "THE SECOND COMING OF JESUS"

1. How do you feel about the state of the world today? Does it seem worse, better or the same as it's always been? Why?

2. How would you respond to a friend who says, "Look, after two thou-

sand years I think it's safe to assume that Jesus isn't going to come back. Maybe Jesus meant it as a figure of speech rather than a literal promise"?

3. Have you ever run into a view of the end times that doesn't seem to square with what the Bible says? What was it, and how did it compare to what you learned in *The Essential Jesus*?

4. What's your rationale for making things better in the here and now, since God is going to create a new heaven and a new earth anyway?

5. Some Christians say that in light of the return of Christ the only thing that matters is evangelism, and that we shouldn't waste too much time on things like peace, justice, poverty and the environment. What do you say?

6. What is your view of heaven? What will it be like, who will be there, and how can you be sure you'll be one of them?

7. In what ways does your view of the second coming of Jesus affect the way you live today?

Who Is Jesus . . . to You?

WHEN I WAS GROWING UP, we had a tradition in our home that I didn't like very much. Each year on Good Friday, from noon until 3 p.m., my mother would make me and my siblings go to our rooms and write out the answer to this question: Who is Jesus to you? I knew the reason she made us do this is because those were the hours that Jesus hung on the cross: "It was now about the sixth hour, and darkness came over the whole land until the ninth hour" (Luke 23:44).

But I didn't like it because at that time of the year it was just starting to get warm, and I always wanted to be outside playing baseball. It seemed that on every Good Friday the weather was perfect for baseball. But usually, in spite of my grumpy attitude at first, when I finally sat down to write my answer, it became one of the most meaningful things I did all year. I'm a grown man now, with children and grandchildren of my own, but I still get by myself on Good Friday from noon until 3 p.m. and write in my journal about Jesus. I love to remind myself of how much he has done for me.

In our next section you'll have an opportunity to examine the experiences of five people who had encounters with Jesus. The rich young man walked away from Jesus because he loved his money. Nicodemus didn't believe Jesus at first, but over time, he became a follower. Once the woman at the well got over her shame, she accepted Jesus as her Savior. Saul had a dramatic encounter with Jesus that changed his life, and the world, forever. And Peter gave a stunning affirmation of Jesus even though he didn't yet understand all that it would cost him. But the thread that holds them all together is that each person had to make a personal decision about Jesus.

At the beginning of this book, I told you I'm a follower of Jesus but that your decision about him was your responsibility. I simply wanted to guide you through one hundred Bible passages about Jesus and then leave it to you to come to your own conclusion. I'm still going to stick with that. But I will tell you this: my hope and prayer is that if you haven't yet made your decision to believe in Jesus and follow him, you will do so by the end of this book. (If you'd like some help with that, you can refer to "How to Begin a Relationship with Jesus Christ" on pp. 197-98.)

One last thing: as I've written this book, I've truly enjoyed taking a journey through the Bible's greatest story myself. And I hope that as you've read, reflected and prayed your way through the hundred stops on that same journey, you've not only gotten an appreciation for the essential Jesus but also developed a love for prayerfully reading God's Word. But don't let this book be the end of your times in the Bible. Let it become the beginning of a lifetime of meeting God every day in the Bible and prayer.

96 ❦ THE RICH DO-GOODER

PRAY: Lord, I ask that you clear my mind and heart of every distraction so that I can have a fresh encounter with you today.

READ: Matthew 19:16-30

REFLECT: Over the years, I've heard some people, usually those with lots of money, express frustration with the story in Matthew 19:16-30: "Well, I guess we're all supposed to give away everything and live like St. Francis, is that it?" I've also heard other people, usually those who wish they had more money, express satisfaction with this passage, "Well, I guess rich people don't really understand the gospel, do they?" But a careful reading of what Jesus said reveals that he was talking not only about money and possessions but also about something far more serious.

Notice that the rich man's ice-breaker was about eternal life (v. 16). In spite of all his wealth in this world, he was worried about what would happen to him in the next. That's still the "big issue." Regardless of who you are, who you know or how much you've accomplished in life, at some point everyone must come to grips with this question: how do I get to heaven?

The man in this passage thought he had it all figured out: do good things (vv. 16, 20). That's what many people believe today. They imagine a giant cosmic scale, and if your good deeds outweigh your bad, bingo, you're in! But Jesus pulls the rug out from under that perspective. First, he challenges what it means to be good (v. 17). He then carries the philosophy to its logical extension: just being good isn't good enough; to earn your salvation you must be perfect (v. 21). Excuse me? Even the disciples were baffled; if a good, rich man can't get in, who can (v. 25)?

But by the end of the conversation Jesus made it clear there were two things preventing this man from gaining the eternal life he sought: his attachment to wealth *and* his belief that salvation could be earned through good works. The man went away sad (v. 22) because neither of those strategies works. In the end, Jesus made it clear that there is only one way to get to heaven: "Follow me" (vv. 21, 28). That means believing in Jesus and living like him, and he had been saying that all along.

APPLY: Are there things that prevent you from completely following Jesus? If so, what are they, and what would it take for you to remove them?

PRAY: Spend a few minutes talking to Jesus, imagining that he has personally addressed this challenge to you: "Follow me."

97 ❧ THE BOTTOM LINE

PRAY: Lord, in addition to knowing about you, please show me how I can have a relationship with you as I read your Word today.

READ: John 3:1-21

REFLECT: I've worked in nonprofit organizations all my life, and that's given me many opportunities to try my hand at fundraising. I once telephoned a man I had never met; I was hoping to begin a relationship that would someday lead to a contribution. I had my phone script all prepared, but before I got even a few seconds into it the man cut me off, "What's the bottom line; how much do you want?" Uh . . .

In a way, that's what Jesus does to Nicodemus; he cuts him off and goes to the bottom line: you must be born again (vv. 3, 7). Jesus interrupted Nicodemus's theological script (v. 2) because he wanted to address the real issue: in spite of his high position (v. 1) and religious knowledge (v. 10), Nicodemus was outside of God's kingdom (vv. 3, 5). It reminds us that just going to church or even knowing a lot about the Christian faith does no good unless we've been truly born again.

But what exactly does it mean to be born again? Today, millions of people claim they are. Some think of "born-againers" as unpleasant zealots. Others think of them as a voting block to be manipulated. But Jesus defined them as people who believe that he is the Son of God, the one who died on the cross to save humankind from sin (vv. 14-18). And when a person finally accepts that truth, they begin a whole new life.

That was a lot for Nicodemus to swallow all at once (v. 9), and there's no evidence here that he accepted Jesus' message. But the seed planted that night began to grow; later Nicodemus defended Jesus (John 7:50-51), and finally he publicly identified himself as a follower of Christ (John 19:38-42). Some people put their trust in Jesus the first time they hear the gospel message. For others, believing in Jesus is a process with many steps. But no matter how it happens or how long it takes, the bottom line is this: you must be born again.

APPLY: Where are you in the process of believing in Jesus?

PRAY: Spend a few minutes talking to Jesus, imagining that he has personally addressed this challenge to you: "You must be born again."

98 ❧ No More Shame

PRAY: "I sought the LORD, and he answered me; he delivered me from all my fears. Those who look to him are radiant; their faces are never covered with shame" (Psalm 34:4-5).

READ: John 4:1-42

REFLECT: The woman in our passage today was carrying more than a water jug as she walked to the well; her heart was burdened down with sin and shame. How do we know? First, she was a Samaritan, a group of people who were ostracized by the Jews (v. 9). Next, she was a woman; many at that time, including even Jesus' disciples, would have considered her a second-class citizen (v. 27). Finally, she had lived a sinful life that produced a series of broken relationships (vv. 17-18). No wonder she went by herself in the heat of the day.

Many people today struggle with a deep sense of shame. Some can't forgive themselves for a terrible sin in their past; others have been deeply wounded by someone else's sin. Either way, sin and shame can leave us feeling broken, unworthy and alone. But sometimes our lowest moment is when we are closest to God (Psalm 34:18).

That's what happened to this woman. She met Jesus, and he used the encounter to change her life forever. First he revealed that he was the source of "living water" (vv. 10, 13-14); she probably thought he meant "running water" from a moving stream. But in fact, he meant the Holy Spirit; that's what Jesus offers to all who follow him. Next he told her that soon all people could have a relationship with God; everyone, not just the Jews, would worship God in spirit and truth (vv. 22-24). But this would only be possible because God's promised Messiah had arrived (vv. 25-26).

By the end of the encounter, the woman accepted Jesus not just as a man (v. 9) or as a prophet (v. 19) but as "the Savior of the world" (v. 42). And that's what turned her burden of sin and shame into a source of joy. She could invite her friends to meet the man "who told me everything I ever did" (vv. 29, 39) because he had forgiven her. And that joy is available to everyone who believes in Jesus today.

APPLY: How would you feel if you met someone who knew all your darkest secrets?

PRAY: Lord, you know everything I've ever done. I ask that you would forgive me and then fill me with your living water.

99 ❧ ANGRY YOUNG MAN

PRAY: Heavenly Father, I ask that you enable me to see one or two things I can do to draw closer to you.

READ: Acts 9:1-19

REFLECT: Saul was an angry young man (Acts 7:58). He hated Christians (Acts 9:1) and tracked them down to throw them into prison (v. 2). So much for religious tolerance. But Saul's vendetta raises an interesting question: Why does Jesus make some people so mad? For some it has to do with their unwillingness to give up a particular lifestyle. Others feel they've been betrayed by a Christian loved one. Still others can't accept Jesus' claim to be the only way to God (John 14:6).

But often, all of these reactions are a smoke screen for a deeper issue: External anger at Jesus can be a clue that an internal spiritual struggle is going on. That seems to be the case with Saul. There was no question about his passion for God. Elsewhere in the Bible we learn that he devoted his life to Judaism; he was a model Pharisee (Acts 23:6; 2 Corinthians 11:21-22). But when Saul literally "saw the light," it burned off all his anger. He still had questions (Acts 9:5), but until he let go of the anger he couldn't hear the answers. That's true for us as well.

I've heard some Christians apologize for the fact that "my testimony is not that dramatic," as if the only way to be truly converted is to get knocked to the ground and to hear the voice of Jesus. Sometimes conversion is immediate and dramatic, and we can thank God for the times he chooses to work that way.

But more often, conversion is a gradual process where a person comes to faith in Jesus over time. Even Saul's conversion demonstrates this: he grew up in a religious environment, developed a passion for God, had a dramatic encounter with Jesus, but then received support from the Christian community in Damascus (vv. 17-19). It took all these steps to transform the angry young man into God's chosen instrument who could preach that Jesus is the Son of God (vv. 15, 20).

APPLY: What is the next step you could take in your relationship with Jesus?

PRAY: Ask Jesus for the courage to take next step in your relationship with him.

100 ❧ THE ESSENTIAL JESUS CHALLENGE

PRAY: Heavenly Father, I thank you for everything you've taught me during my journey through the Bible. Please show me anything else you want me to know before it comes to an end.

READ: Luke 9:18-27

REFLECT: When I was in high school my pastor invited me to share my testimony in front of the entire church. I agreed because I had grown up in a Christian home and I felt confident I knew what to say. But when the day finally arrived and I stepped to the front, I suddenly realized the challenge wasn't just to say what my pastor or my parents or anyone else wanted to hear. With the eyes of everyone staring at me, I had to say what I really believed about Jesus.

It's that kind of fish-or-cut-bait moment that the disciples have reached in Luke 9. As a result of Jesus' preaching, parables and miracles, everyone is talking about him. So Jesus asks a general question, "Who do the crowds say I am?" (v. 18). Most people today would be comfortable with that one; they could simply repeat what they've heard from others, which is exactly what the disciples did (v. 19).

But Jesus didn't come to earth to help people memorize a textbook answer about himself. He came so that everyone could have a personal relationship with him. So he presses the point; perhaps this is what he had been praying about earlier (v. 18). "Who do *you* say I am?" (v. 20); that's the essential Jesus challenge. And it is Peter, the impulsive fisherman, who rises to the challenge: "You are the Christ, the Son of the living God" (Matthew 16:16; see Luke 9:20). The disciples still had a lot to learn about Jesus, and a lot to go through with him (Luke 9:21-27). But they had crossed a threshold in their relationship with Jesus.

As we've discovered in our journey through the Bible, what you believe about Jesus is the most important issue you'll ever face. My prayer is that you'll join Peter and countless millions throughout the ages who have affirmed with all their hearts, "You are the Christ, the Son of the living God," because when you do, you will have crossed the threshold into eternal life.

APPLY: What do you really believe about Jesus?

PRAY: Spend a few minutes talking to Jesus, imagining that he has personally addressed his challenge to you: "Who do *you* say that I am?"

DISCUSSION QUESTIONS FOR "WHO IS JESUS . . . TO YOU?"

1. Why do so many people believe that salvation can be earned by doing enough good deeds? Why do so many people struggle with the idea that salvation is a free gift from God?

2. Jesus said you cannot serve both God and money (Matthew 6:24).

How is that possible in our modern world? How can we know when we've crossed the line, that we love money and possessions too much?

3. For Nicodemus, coming to faith in Jesus was a process. What have been the steps in your process for discovering who Jesus is? How long has it taken, and what do you think the next step might be?

4. The woman at the well was struggling with her sense of shame. Have you ever felt like negative experiences in your past were holding you back from drawing closer to God? What happened?

5. Early in his life, Saul was an angry person. Have you ever had a phase in your life when you've been angry at God? Why? Were you able to resolve the source of your anger? How?

6. Peter boldly declared his belief in Jesus. Have you ever been in a situation where you had to publicly explain what you believe about Jesus? What happened? Do you remember the first time you spoke up for Jesus?

7. Who is Jesus to you?

How to Begin a Relationship with Jesus Christ

AS YOU'VE DISCOVERED IN *THE ESSENTIAL JESUS*, the greatest story in the Bible is that God made a way for you to have a real relationship with him through Jesus Christ. That may sound attractive to you, but you may ask, "How do I begin?" Here's how:

- *Admit* that you have sinned and that your sins have separated you from God.

- *Believe* that Jesus is the Son of God, who died on the cross to pay for your sins and give you new life.

- *Decide* to follow Jesus for the rest of your life.

Here's a simple prayer that you (or a friend) might say to begin a life-long relationship with Jesus.

> Dear God, I admit that I've done wrong things and that my sin has separated me from you. I believe you sent your Son Jesus to earth to die for the sins of the world—including mine—and that you brought him back to life again. Lord Jesus, as of right now I'm deciding to follow you every day. Holy Spirit, I ask for your help to live a new life. Amen!

ABOUT YOUR NEW LIFE

Once you begin a relationship with God through Jesus Christ, you'll want make it grow. Here are some ideas for how you can do that.

- *Talk to God.* That means prayer. You can talk to God any time, either silently or out loud. God loves to hear from you.

- *Listen to God.* The best way is by reading the Bible; you'll come to know God better and understand how he wants you to live.

- *Join a church.* You need the support of other believers. Find a church where the people love Jesus and believe the Bible, and you'll begin to grow.

May God bless you!

THE ESSENTIAL JESUS CHALLENGE
An Exploration of the Bible's Greatest Story
For Churches and Groups

Imagine the impact of having your entire church, Sunday school or home-group network reading and discussing the Bible's greatest story—together. That's what *The Essential Jesus Challenge* is all about.

Based on the book *The Essential Jesus*, the Challenge guides participants through the list of short Bible passages following the story line of Jesus Christ—25 from the Old Testament and 75 from the New Testament—over a twenty-week period. The program is undated and designed to be flexible; it fits any time schedule and works with any Bible translation.

Scripture Union has produced a leader's kit that includes a how-to guide, posters, banners, bulletin inserts and everything you need to make *The Essential Jesus Challenge* an effective churchwide Bible engagement experience. The leader's kit also includes ideas for making the Challenge a Bible-based evangelistic outreach into your community.

For more information, go to **www.EssentialJesusChallenge.com** or call Scripture Union at **1-610-935-2807**.

About Scripture Union

Since 1868, Scripture Union has been involved in Bible engagement and children's outreach ministries and today is active in 130 countries worldwide. In the United States, Scripture Union has several Bible engagement programs and publications for all ages, including *Encounter with God®*, *Discovery®* and *The Essential 100 Challenge,* as well as a variety of evangelism and discipleship programs for children, including SuperKids® outreach missions and PrimeTime® after school programs.

For more information, go to **www.ScriptureUnion.org** or call **1-610-935-2807**.